USING THE BOOCH METHOD:
A RATIONAL APPROACH

USING THE BOOCH METHOD:
A RATIONAL APPROACH

ISEULT WHITE

The Benjamin/Cummings Publishing Company, Inc.
Redwood City, California • Menlo Park, California
Reading, Massachusetts • New York • Don Mills, Ontario
Wokingham, U.K. • Amsterdam • Bonn • Sydney
Singapore • Tokyo • Madrid • San Juan

Executive Editor: Dan Joraanstad
Editorial Assistant: Melissa Standen
Production Editor: Teri Holden
Marketing Manager: Mary Tudor
Manufacturing Coordinator: Janet Weaver
Cover Design: Yvo Riezebos
Text Design & Composition: London Road Design
Copy Editor: Barbara Conway
Proofreader: Eleanor Renner Brown
Indexer: Ruthanne Lowe

Many of the designations used by manufacturers and sellers to distinguish their products are claimed as trademarks. Where those designations appear in this book, and Benjamin/Cummings was aware of a trademark claim, the designations have been printed in initial caps or all caps.

Booch Components is a registered trademark of Grady Booch; FrameMaker and Frame Technology are registered trademarks of Frame Technology Corporation; FrameWriter, FrameViewer, FrameMath, Frame, and the Frame logo are trademarks of Frame Technology Corporation; Rational and Rational Rose are registered trademarks of Rational. All rights reserved. Windows is a trademark of Microsoft Corporation.

Printed in the United States of America.

Library of Congress Cataloging-in-Publication Data
White, Iseult.
    Using the Booch method : a rational method / Iseult White.
        p.   cm.
    Includes index.
    ISBN 0-8053-0614-5
    1. Computer software—Development.   I. Title.
QA76.76.D47W483 1994
005.1'2—dc20   94-701
                                            CIP

ISBN 0-8053-0614-5
1 2 3 4 5 6 7 8 9 10-CRS-98 97 96 95 94
The Benjamin/Cummings Publishing Company, Inc.
390 Bridge Parkway
Redwood City, CA 94065

FOR JOE,
AGUS AN BUACHAILL BÓ,
THANK YOU FOR EVERYTHING.

Foreword

THE DEMAND FOR increasingly sophisticated software-intensive systems continues to grow unabated. The fact that advances in hardware continue to outpace the industry's ability to develop quality software, coupled with society's growing reliance on automation, together make the software developer's work both urgent and interesting.

Object-oriented technology has proven itself useful in the engineering of such quality software systems. Object-oriented programming languages such as C++, Smalltalk, and Ada9x have evolved to address the tactical issues of implementing automated solutions. Standards for object-oriented databases, user interfaces, and distributed object managers have begun to emerge, each addressing some different functional aspect of a software system. Finally, object-oriented analysis methods have sprung up to guide the analyst and end user in expressing a system's desired behavior. Similarly, object-oriented design methods have been developed to aid the architect and programmer in crafting a system's solution.

The Booch method is perhaps the most mature and widely-used of these object-oriented analysis and design methods. Since its beginnings in the early 1980's, this method has grown to embrace the practices of many successful projects, and so provides a framework for a repeatable, mature software development process. Thousands of projects world-wide have now employed this method to successfully develop and deliver complex software systems.

Iseult White is one of the more experienced practitioners of the Booch method. As my colleague at Rational, she has taught the method to hundreds of managers and developers and has applied the method in engagements ranging from embedded applications to enterprise-wide computing systems. *Using the Booch Method: A Rational Approach* thus provides an approachable and pragmatic guide to the use of the Booch method in creating quality software-intensive systems.

Grady Booch

January 1994

Preface

GOALS

THIS BOOK PROVIDES practical guidance on the construction of systems using the Booch method of software development. Its specific goals are

- To provide a sound understanding of the fundamental principles of the Booch method

- To give examples of the usage of the key elements of the Booch notation

- To teach the application of the Booch method by using a sample problem domain

AUDIENCE

THIS BOOK IS written for the computer professional as well as for the student. It is suitable for use in professional seminars and individual study as well as in undergraduate and graduate courses. It shows you how to

- Use the Booch method effectively to solve real problems

- Develop a system from requirements to detailed design by using object-oriented analysis and design

Since this is a case study using the Booch method of object-oriented design, you should already have a general understanding of the Booch method, its specialized terms, and its notation, or be in the process of learning about the method.[1] This book also assumes some familiarity with basic software engineering concepts.

---

[1] Grady Booch, *Object-Oriented Analysis and Design with Applications.* (Redwood City, CA: Benjamin/Cummings, 1993).

APPROACH

THIS BOOK TAKES a practical approach to teaching the Booch method. It uses a case study to show the analysis and design of a complete application. The application is a simple system that records and scores the results of gymnastics competitions. This problem domain was chosen because it is easily understood and not specific to any field of computer science. The reader can concentrate on the specifics of modeling the domain in the Booch method, rather than investing time in understanding an unfamiliar problem domain. The problem domain is first described in Chapter 2.

The method is described as a number of sequential steps. It gives the new user a framework for developing object-oriented applications and provides advanced techniques for more experienced users. As users become fluent in the method, they will be able to move back and forth through the steps, and often combine several steps, until the desired result is achieved.

A software development method such as the Booch method is best supported by a CASE tool. This book makes use of the CASE tool *Rational Rose 2.0®*. At every step in the method, there is a description of how to use *Rational Rose 2.0* to complete this step. This information is called out in separate text boxes. They are provided as an extra aid to users of *Rational Rose 2.0*. If you are using another CASE tool or simply drawing the diagrams by hand, you can ignore these text boxes. To obtain a copy of *Rational Rose 2.0*, contact Rational Software Corporation, 2800 San Tomas Expressway, Santa Clara, CA 95051-0951, 1-800-767-3237.

STRUCTURE

THIS DOCUMENT IS organized in chapters covering the following topics:

- Overview of the Booch method

- Requirements analysis

- Object-oriented domain analysis

- Object-oriented design

In addition, there are two appendices.

Overview
Chapter 1 establishes the principles of the Booch method. It summarizes the steps of the method, and discusses the deliverables of each step.

Requirements Analysis
Chapter 2 discusses possible sources of information on the requirements of the system and shows the creation of a system function statement and system charter. It also describes the problem domain of the Gymnastics System used throughout the book.

Object-oriented Domain Analysis
Chapters 3 through 7 describe the steps of domain analysis in detail. Chapter 3 discusses how to find, define, and document key abstractions (classes) of the domain. Chapter 4 illustrates the definition of key associations or dependencies between classes that need to reference or contain information from other classes. Chapter 5 shows how to represent the behavior of the system through the definition of operations for each class. Chapter 6 examines the identification of attributes and their assignment to the appropriate classes. It also discusses the discovery of generalized classes, or supertypes, and of specialized classes, or subclasses. Finally, Chapter 7 presents ways to validate an analysis model.

Object-oriented Design
Chapters 8, 9, and 10 describe the transformation of an analysis model into a design model. Chapter 8 explains the basic concepts of system design. Chapter 9 shows how to organize the design into a structured architecture, and how to plan for the iterative refinement of the design through the building of successive executable releases of implementation. Chapter 10 examines the typical steps involved in the construction of each executable release.

Appendices

Finally, there are two appendices. Appendix A provides the complete documentation of the Gymnastics System as developed using *Rational Rose 2.0*. Appendix B gives a detailed definition of the Booch notation.

USING THIS BOOK

THIS MANUAL CAN be read straight through to obtain the fundamental concepts of the Booch method, and a sense of how the object-oriented software engineering process works. It can also be used together with *Rational Rose 2.0*. Using it in this manner will allow you to work some of the examples for yourself and develop a more detailed understanding of the Booch method.

ACKNOWLEDGMENTS

A NUMBER OF individuals have contributed to my understanding of software development using the Booch method. For their ideas and help I especially thank Glenn Andert, John Berry, Rob Brownsword, Grady Booch, Marc Goldberg, Peter Goubert, Doug Hill, Phil Levy, Dave Stephenson, Daryl Winters, and Robert Yerex. I would also like to thank Jennifer Fell, Andrea Frankel, Marie Novicki, and Lori Stipp for their contributions to the style, presentation, and writing of this book. Finally I would like to thank my management at Rational Software Corporation for their support of this work—in particular, Mark Frappier and Ron Lang for their patience and encouragement during this project.

Contents

Preface   ix

CHAPTER 1
Overview of the Booch Method   1
    Definition of the Booch Method   3
    The Steps of the Booch Method   6
    Requirements Analysis   6
    Domain Analysis   9
    System Design   11
    Glossary   14

CHAPTER 2
Requirements Analysis   17
    The Role of Requirements Analysis   19
    Finding Sources of Requirements   19
    The Gymnastics System's Requirements   22
    The System Charter   24
    The System Function Statement   24
    Summary: Progress So Far   25
    Glossary   25

CHAPTER 3
Domain Analysis: Defining Classes   27
    Identifying Key Classes   29
    Identifying Key Abstractions
      in the Gymnastics System   33
    Summary: Progress So Far   40

CHAPTER 4
Domain Analysis: Relationships   41
    Relationships   43

Refining Relationships   47
Defining Cardinality of Relationships   48
Summary: Progress So Far   51
Glossary   52

CHAPTER 5
Domain Analysis: Defining Operations   53
General Approaches to Assigning Operations   55
Modeling Use Cases   56
Operations Required for Each Class   58
Summary: Progress So Far   60

CHAPTER 6
Domain Analysis: Attributes and Inheritance   61
Defining Attributes   63
General Approaches to Attribution   64
Assigning Attributes to Classes   66
Defining Inheritance   67
Identifying Superclasses   68
Identifying Subclasses   69
Summary: Progress So Far   70
Glossary   71

CHAPTER 7
Domain Analysis: Validation and Iteration   73
Validating the Model   75
Iterating   77
Summary: Iterating Through the Cycle   80

CHAPTER 8
System Design: Overview   83
Definition of Design   85

Principles of Design   85
Steps of Design   88
Products of Design   93
Glossary   94

CHAPTER 9

System Design: Initial Architecture   95
              Defining an Architecture   97
              Choosing Major Service Software   97
              Defining Class Categories   98
              Summary: Progress So Far   104
              Glossary   105

CHAPTER 10

System Design: Developing an Executable Release   107
              Building an Executable Release   109
              The Steps of Design   110
              Adding Control Classes   111
              Detailing the Implementation of Operations   112
              Adding Navigational Paths   116
              Implementing Relationships   116
              Defining Access Control   119
              Summary: Developing an Executable Release   121
              Glossary   121

APPENDIX A   123
APPENDIX B   171
Index   205

Chapter 1

Overview of the Booch Method

Definition of the Booch Method

The Steps of the Booch Method

Requirements Analysis

Domain Analysis

System Design

Glossary

DEFINITION OF THE BOOCH METHOD

THE BOOCH METHOD is a software-development method used to develop and communicate the design of a system that will be implemented primarily in software.

A software-development method is a standardized means of presenting and communicating the requirements of a system and the design decisions. This provides an effective means of delivering those requirements to a customer.

The Booch method is an object-oriented method based on proven heuristics for developing quality software that not only provides an effective design but also supports that design and the development of future systems.

In an object-oriented method, the basic unit of design is the object, typically a recognizable real-world structure or an **abstraction** based on that structure. This allows the software to maintain a one-to-one mapping with the real world. Compared to systems designed using previous software-development methods, these designs

- Are more able to flex as the world, or the understanding of it, changes

- Provide units that fit the environment rather than a specific system, and apply to any system dealing with that part of the environment

- Make the system easier to understand, and thus to maintain, by both customers and software developers

The object-oriented approach is not a radical new perspective or means of doing systems development. Rather it is an outgrowth of the work done in systems engineering over the last 30 years. It maintains the sound concepts of information hiding, coupling, and cohesion.

Object-oriented design provides a **model** to support solid analysis and design, and it allows the developers and implementors to enhance, correct, and maintain the same consistent model from the beginning of analysis through coding and implementation.

The increased interest in and popularity of object-oriented methods over the last five years speaks for the solid principles behind the concepts. The popularity of the Booch method shows that it can provide the expressive notation, practicality, and working heuristics needed by businesses that must produce working systems efficiently and cost-effectively to harness the power of an object-oriented design.

Producing a Model

A method is more than its notation. Users of the Booch method develop models of a system and then directly implement these models in units of working code, known as **executable releases.** These executable releases are true subsets of the final working code, not the "quick-hack" throwaway simulations often used to supplement other methods. Each recognizable portion of the Booch method (a diagram, a specification, or an actual executable release) is a view of an underlying, fully integrated model of the system as it finally will be implemented.

The model is built in stages that allow for concentration on certain aspects of a system at a given time. Much as an architect draws various plans, views, and schematics for the building of a skyscraper, the choice of diagrams allows focus on critical areas of the system. The result is a series of clear, expressive presentations aimed at answering specific questions about the systems design or requirements. The decisions made based on these presentations are then captured in the underlying model.

Improving Productivity by Using Practical Models

The Booch method is not the first software-development method to develop a model. However, many developers have had the negative experience of developing extensive models of systems, only to find that they were effective in theory but so abstract that they could not be implemented in code.

Developers using the Booch method do not develop throwaway work or work that must undergo massive, sometimes mysterious, conversions before being implemented in real code. Instead, through an incremental approach that permits selective focus and concentration, they can contribute real pieces of design that, if found in review to be well done and working in executable releases, will appear in the end product. This allows the application of strong development theory to real products without the added overhead of abstractions that do not appear in the final design, as occurs in some software-development methods.

Taking an Iterative Approach

Booch has adopted a practical approach to procedures and deliverables. Developers recognize that the discovery process needed for thorough understanding of requirements, services, devices, and system software cannot be neatly boxed into fixed stages.

In the past, many methods used in software development insisted on a rigid series of steps: Classically, first you discovered everything you needed to know about analysis, then everything you needed to know about design, and so on.

The Booch method allows for the reality that the development of a system is an iterative process—previous work must always be added to or refined as the results of that work are used in the next stage of development.

An iterative approach still has the classic steps—that is, developers look at requirements first and then map them to design. However, as developers continually integrate their discoveries into one underlying model, they can easily move back and forth between analysis and design. In fact, the method specifically encourages early coding of pieces of the system to aid in the requirements-discovery process. The design should allow for change and discovery as the development process continues.

At the same time, good project management requires focused deliverables and a recommended sequence of activities. So the

Booch method presents a set of steps that may look, at first glance, like a classic waterfall method. The difference is that this is a "mini" set of steps that is applied iteratively to pieces of a system. In practice, developers analyze a little, design a little, and code a little. Then they cycle back and do it again, only on more of the system. All of analysis, design, and coding are accomplished, but in a series of cycles rather than three large leaps.

The decisions on how large each cycle must be are left to the project planners of the development effort; the method allows the flexibility to be as fixed or cyclic as the designers and managers prefer. However, some advice on choosing executable releases to develop is offered later in this book.

THE STEPS OF THE BOOCH METHOD

AS SHOWN IN Figure 1-1 on page 7, the Booch method consists of three steps:

- *Requirements analysis*, which provides the basic charter for the system's functions

- *Domain analysis*, which provides the key logical structure of the system

- *System design*, which provides the key physical structure of the system, maps the logical structure to it, and leads to working executable releases

REQUIREMENTS ANALYSIS

REQUIREMENTS ANALYSIS IS the process of determining what the customer wants a system to do. It is a high-level stage that identifies the key functions the system is to perform, defines the scope of the domain that the system will support, and documents the key practices and policies of the enterprise that the system must support.

Use case analysis, first formalized by Jacobson,[1] is a very power-ful method of describing system functions. Jacobson defines a **use case** as "a particular form or pattern or exemplar of usage, a sce-nario that begins with some user of the system initiating some transaction or sequence of interrrelated events." In a flight reserva-tion system, the action of reserving a flight would be a use case. Each use case describes some way of using the system. The col-lected use cases specify the complete functionality of the system.

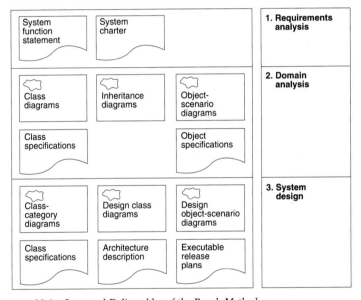

Figure 1-1 Major Steps and Deliverables of the Booch Method

During requirements analysis, the analyst works with end users and domain experts to enumerate the use cases that are key to the system's operation. These use cases are used throughout domain analysis and design for finding classes and operations, validation, and testing.

---

[1] Ivar Jacobson, *Object-Oriented Software Engineering, A Use Case Driven Approach* (Reading, MA: Addison-Wesley, 1992). See Chapter 7 for a discus-sion of use case analysis.

Objective

Requirements analysis essentially forms a contract between the customer and the developers on what the system is to provide for the customer. This contract is not fixed; as the development cycle continues, it will be changed often. It does serve as a starting point and central reference for what the system is supposed to do.

Deliverables

The method requires two formal products from this stage:

- *System charter,* which outlines the responsibilities of the system

- *System function statement,* which outlines the key use cases of the system

During this phase, it is common to develop sketches of key inputs and outputs of the system, or a list of references to key statements of policy, existing systems and procedures, and so on. Many companies and agencies require other statements of requirements in a particular format that would be considered deliverables of this phase.

Steps

No formal steps are defined for requirements analysis because this process varies dramatically depending on the newness of the system, the availability and level of agreement of the customers and policy experts, and the availability of additional documents (feasibility studies, project charters, and so on) that explain what the system is supposed to accomplish. Requirements analysis can be as simple as the review and synopsis of a recommendation for the development of a system. It can also be as demanding, complex, and time consuming as the development of a single charter through the interview, consensus building, and negotiation process of hundreds of individuals and agencies with an interest in a single project.

Participants

Quality requirements analysis depends on the teamwork of knowledgeable experts, policy holders, economic managers, negotiators, and clear communicators.

DOMAIN ANALYSIS

DOMAIN ANALYSIS IS the process of defining a precise, concise, and object-oriented model of that part of the real-world enterprise that is relevant to the system (the problem domain). It is through this process that the developers gain the detailed knowledge of the problem domain needed to create a system capable of carrying out the required functions. During a later stage, the system domain also assumes importance.

Objective

Domain analysis identifies all major objects in the domain, including all data and major operations that will be needed to carry out the system's function.

Domain analysts produce a central model containing all the semantics of the system in a set of concise but detailed definitions. This process focuses on resolving a potentially bewildering range of vocabulary used to describe the system, contradictory requirements, obscure policy, and varying styles of explanation and communication into a standardized presentation and structure that will map directly to final implementation.

Good domain analysis also adds appropriate levels of abstraction to a system. With careful analysis and definition of the domain areas, structures can be built that will be directly reusable in many systems that overlap this area of an enterprise. This broader perspective, without appreciably expanding the time to produce the system, will increase the speed of development and quality of future systems and allow for flexibility and change of the system during both its development and its productive life.

Deliverables

The deliverables of domain analysis include

- *Class diagrams,* which identify the key classes, or types, of the domain

- *Class specifications,* which contain all semantic definitions of the classes, their relationships, their attributes, and their key operations

- *Object-scenario diagrams,* which illustrate how the objects will interact to carry out key system functions

- *Data dictionary,* which lists all the domain entities including classes, relationships, and attributes

These are various presentations of a single underlying model that will contain the definition of all classes, objects, relationships, and so on of the logical portion of the system.

Steps

The following steps are performed during domain analysis:

- *Define classes,* which includes identifying the major types of domain objects and defining them

- *Define relationships,* which includes describing major associations between those objects

- *Define operations,* which includes identifying the major operations required to support class structure and system functions

- *Find attributes,* which includes determining the properties that describe the classes

- *Define inheritance,* which includes finding generalizations and specializations within similar domain types

- *Validate and iterate,* which includes the review, testing, and repair of the model and actually occurs throughout the process

This is a highly iterative process—that is, key abstractions may not appear until you define key mechanisms, or you may discover some inheritance when you find attributes. These steps are only recommended approaches, not fixed requirements for successful analysis.

Participants

Domain analysis is a first marriage of systems and domain expertise. Generally a software engineer or architect's knowledge of good abstraction and the semantics of an object-oriented system is required to produce the deliverables. However, sound semantic definition of the classes and their relationships, knowledge of required calculations and processing, and knowledge of required data (attributes) and their meaning requires domain expertise often found only at the customer site. Domain analysis cannot be done in isolation. The products can be produced by customers or systems analysts schooled in object-oriented design, even if they are not technical experts on software implementation.

Frequently these deliverables are produced by a small team of domain experts and software engineers who have strong customer communication skills.

SYSTEM DESIGN

Design is the process of determining effective, efficient, and cost-effective implementation to carry out the functions and store the data defined in domain analysis.

Objectives

During design, the appropriate computers, devices, software services, system software, software units, and data storage strategies required for system development are selected.

Design maps the "ideal" or logical analysis product developed during domain analysis to a structure that will allow these objects and classes to be coded and executed.

Producing design models allows the expertise of many software engineers to be shared to achieve validation of design decisions.

Deliverables

The model that was started in analysis is the core of the design model. Design adds the following:

- *Architectural descriptions,* which capture major design decisions such as choice of processors, database managers, operating systems, language, and so on

- *Executable release descriptions,* which define the goals and content of successive executable release implementations to focus on and test the design and requirements

- *Class-category diagrams,* which model the partitioning of the system into high-level groupings of classes and objects

- *Design class diagrams,* which show the abstractions of the physical implementation, detailed data types and structures, and the mapping of the logical abstractions to the physical abstractions

- *Design object-scenario diagrams,* which show the detailed operational logic which carries out a function, including the use of the physical objects

- *New specifications* supporting these diagrams

- *Amended class specifications* showing full operational specifications for those operations with complex algorithms, the implementation of relationships, and the typing of attributes

Steps

The following steps are performed during design:

- *Determine the initial architecture,* which includes making decisions on the high-level implementation resources and services, the class categories to be used, and the executable releases to be developed

- *Plan executable releases,* which includes the definition of the executable releases

- *Develop executable releases,* which includes the development of classes, detailing of operations, and decisions on public versus private access to objects

- *Refine the design,* which includes folding in what has been learned from executable releases and modifying the design to meet any performance requirements

Like analysis, design is an iterative and incremental process. During design, you can expect to return to analysis when you discover ambiguities or omissions in the analysis model. You will also iterate through the steps of design many times as you build new executable releases, integrate parts of the system, or add to existing executable releases to build a completed system.

Participants

Design is a science requiring engineers schooled in both the technical aspects of developing software and object-oriented design and programming. They must be familiar with all services and with the programming and target operational environments. Top-level architectures are usually the product of the most senior member or members of a software-development staff. Lower-level details can be left to more junior programmers and engineers.

Customers and domain experts are not the primary participants in design, but they must be available to provide final details on the domain needed during logical design, to test and use executable releases, to make any necessary trade-offs on requirements versus performance, and to aid in the iterations back through analysis that are certain to occur.

GLOSSARY

ABSTRACTION

The essential characteristics of an object that distinguish it from all other kinds of objects and thus provide crisply defined conceptual boundaries relative to the perspective of the viewer.

ATTRIBUTE

A property of an object.

CLASS

A set of objects that share a common structure and behavior.

CLASS DIAGRAM

Part of the notation of the Booch method, used to show the existence of classes and their relationships in the logical design of a system. A single class diagram represents a view into the class structure of the system.

CLASS SPECIFICATION

A product of the Booch method used to provide the complete definition of an entity, such as a class, association, or operation

DATA DICTIONARY

A repository for all domain entities including classes, relationships, attributes, and operations that are discovered during analysis and design.

EXECUTABLE RELEASE

A fully executable subset of the final working code of a system.

INHERITANCE

A relationship among classes wherein one class shares the structure or behavior defined in one or more other classes.

MODEL

The set of information that includes a collection of classes, objects, relationships, modules, states, and so on that, taken together, are a consistent and complete description of the system being built.

OBJECT-SCENARIO DIAGRAM

Part of the Booch notation used to illustrate a trace of system execution.

OPERATION

Some behavior that a class makes available to its clients.

RELATIONSHIP

The way in which two classes are associated.

USE CASE

A sequence of actions that constitutes some specific way of using a system.

Chapter 2

Requirements Analysis

■

The Role of Requirements Analysis

■

Finding Sources of Requirements

■

The Gymnastics System's Requirements

■

The System Charter

■

The System Function Statement

■

Summary: Progress So Far

■

Glossary

THE ROLE OF REQUIREMENTS ANALYSIS

NO METHOD, NOTATION, or magic can tell developers what a system is supposed to do. Part of any software-development method will include the careful analysis and information gathering required to determine the customer requirements.

Requirements analysis is done with the customer. The products of requirements analysis are

- *A system charter,* which defines the scope, or boundary, for the system

- *A system function statement,* which provides a high-level statement of what the system must do

FINDING SOURCES OF REQUIREMENTS

THERE ARE NO predefined inputs to this process or a fixed series of steps. Each system differs in its sources of definition. Good requirements definition requires a thorough understanding of the domain in general and the customer needs that this system will satisfy.

Learning the General Domain

Requirements analysis requires the analyst to be very familiar with the domain of the system. That learning process cannot be simulated in this document, but here are some suggestions.

If you are not already familiar with the general vocabulary of the domain, you should do some homework to understand your customer and quickly learn the specific details required for this system.

Do not try to become a domain expert unless you have several years to prepare for this. Try instead to become a knowledgeable layperson. Here are some possibilities for general background:

- Find a good encyclopedia and read the appropriate sections.

- Read the definitive works in the problem domain. The customer can probably point you in the right direction.

- Obtain and read a basic textbook on the subject.

Learning the System Requirements

Even if you are familiar with the domain, you must be certain that you understand the customer's needs for a specific system. To do this requires studying any existing systems (including noncomputerized ones) that are to be replaced or enhanced by the new system. It also requires thorough familiarization with all documents produced to date regarding this project.

Here are some suggestions:

- *Read all overview documents.* These might include

  - Project charters

  - Previous proposals or analyses

  - Requests for proposal or information

  - Feasibility studies

  - Customer reports or requirements documents

  - Previous requests for enhancement or maintenance of existing systems

  - Error reports of existing systems

- *Observe the real thing.* If this were a real system rather than a case study, for example, you might attend gymnastics competitions to find out

  - Who is involved?

  - What equipment is used?

  - What papers do people carry around and how is the information used?

  - What information is used to tune the process?

- *Consult with domain experts.* A domain expert generally is someone who has significant experience actually doing the real thing your system is modeling. In this case study, domain experts could be the meet and team organizers, the judges, and the athletes. If you were writing a manufacturing tracking system, you would choose someone who has worked on the factory floor, understands how to keep the process running efficiently, and has a deep understanding of how an automated system might help improve the manufacturing process.

- *Reuse analysis results from earlier projects.* Perhaps you have solved similar problems before. These earlier results may contain a wealth of useful information. If the previous project used object-oriented analysis or produced data models for a database management system, you may be able to borrow many useful concepts and avoid reinventing the wheel.

- *Check other systems in the same problem domain.* You may have larger or somewhat different goals. Nevertheless, these older systems may address many of the problems that you now face, and related systems may overlap.

- *Build executable releases.* Sometimes you cannot get the information you need from the previously mentioned sources. This may happen because the information does not exist or the cost of getting the information is prohibitive. In this case, you must get the information that you need by building an executable release and getting real data as feedback from running the executable release, preferably with the customer.

Gathering a wide set of resources for information will aid the requirements analyst in this phase and will serve as a continuing source of information for developers and testers.

THE GYMNASTICS SYSTEM'S REQUIREMENTS

The Problem Statement

SINCE IT IS not possible to package real users or old systems in this book, a simple problem statement has been written as the primary source of input.

Figure 2-1 is the problem statement for the case study.

We are about to model a gymnastics scoring system. Our mission is to automate the definition, registration, scoring, and record keeping of a gymnastics season.

Here is a quick description of a gymnastics league and one of their contests: A league is a group of teams that compete against each other. Each team recruits members to participate in the contests.

A typical meet consists of several contests held in the course of one day. For example, there may be a women's all-around, a women's individual, a men's all-around, and so on. There may also be junior and senior competitions. When a team enters a meet, it enters all the competitions. For each contest, each team enters the same number of members, who must compete in all parts of the competition.

Each competition is a series of events run on different equipment. For example, the women's competitions involve balance beam, vault, high bar, and floor exercise. All pieces of equipment are in operation at the same time; each team's competing gymnasts perform on one piece of equipment and then rotate to the next.

Each event has a judging panel assigned to it. These people are qualified scorers for this event. Each judge rates each gymnast on the event and reports the score to a scorekeeper. The scorekeeper throws out the high and low scores and averages the rest. This is the gymnast's score for the event. The team score is the sum of all gymnasts' scores.

Competition scores are the sum of the scores for each of the events. Meet scores are the sum of the competition scores, and so on.

In addition to running the individual meets, the league prepares the schedule of meets for the season, ensures that qualified judges are assigned, registers teams and gymnasts, and publishes seasonal standings.

Figure 2-1 Gymnastics System Problem Statement

Does this description seem a bit vague? It is. When you first start analyzing a project, it is not uncommon for a customer to give you a "wish list" that is similarly vague. There are contradictory documents, numerous aliases, lots of extraneous information, and countless other problems. The resolution of all of this information into a concise, clear specification is the process of analysis.

This problem statement is not meant to be a completely realistic picture of a gymnastics meet; it should be kept simple initially.

Although individual competitions in the real world are run separately and individuals in those competitions do not have to participate in all events or enter an overall competition, that complication is kept out of this picture until later. In this league, for any competition, a team enters a set number of individuals, each of whom competes in every event in the competition, and each of whom, based on their performance in each event, is eligible to compete for the individual overall contest as well as the individual competition in each event. Also, although some events (for example, women's vault) do allow multiple trials in the real world, they get only one chance here.

Keeping it simple at first is not a bad technique in the real world, either. Get the simplest normal situation understood first and then add the complications one at a time.

Sample Outputs

Another source of requirements lies in the desired outputs of the system. Outputs provide not only a major function but also a major source of the data that the system will be managing.

Fully designing all outputs in requirements analysis provides too much detail and leads to too much commitment to an implementation very early in the cycle. However, providing a simple mock-up of key outputs is a worthwhile means of getting key information about the system. This mock-up focuses on the logical content more than the layout of the report.

Figure 2-2 is a sample output of the Gymnastics System.

Meet: Town Invitational
Competition: Women's Senior Team
Date: 12/3/92

	Event Scores			
Club	**Beam**	**Vault**	**Bar**	**Floor**
Flippers	41.5	40.3	44.6	43.7
Acrobats	42.2	38.5	41.0	40.6
Tumblers	37.3	39.8	42.3	41.3
Jugglers	36.8	41.0	37.4	39.6
Page 1				

Figure 2-2 Sample Output of the Gymnastics System

THE SYSTEM CHARTER

A SYSTEM CHARTER is a concise summary of the major responsibilities of a system. It limits the scope of the system and clearly delineates the aspects of gymnastics registration, scoring, and record keeping that will be managed by the first version of the system.

The system charter statement is a simple contract for work; the details are left for other products of analysis and design.

Figure 2-3 is the charter for the Gymnastics System.

System Charter Statement

The Gymnastics System, Release 1.0, will be able to:

■ Record the structure of each meet, including the types of competitions and the types of events in those competitions

■ Keep track of teams and their members, including which members are participating in each competition

■ Keep track of judges, including which type of events they are qualified to judge, which events they are assigned to judge, and the scores they give the gymnasts

■ Maintain a history of the meets and their results

Figure 2-3 Gymnastics System Charter Statement

THE SYSTEM FUNCTION STATEMENT

THE SYSTEM FUNCTION STATEMENT is a summary of the use cases of the system. Each use case describes some piece of functionality or some action that the system must support. It serves these purposes:

- It is used throughout analysis and design to point out needed classes and operations.

- It provides a source of test scenarios to validate that the system meets the requirements.

- It becomes a basis for possible "mini" systems that can be developed as prototypes.

Figure 2-4 is the system function statement for the Gymnastics System.

System Function Statement

■ Register a team in a meet
■ Register a team in a competition
■ Change a gymnast's team membership
■ Assign a judge to an event
■ Score trials, events, and competitions
■ Compute seasonal standings
■ Mail competition schedules to gymnasts and judges

Figure 2-4 The Gymnastics System Function Statement

SUMMARY: PROGRESS SO FAR

AFTER COMPLETING THIS step, you have

■ Started to become familiar with the domain

■ Learned the overall requirements of the system

■ Captured the major functions of the system

You have these deliverables:

■ A system charter (See Figure-2-3)

■ A system function statement (see Figure-2-4)

GLOSSARY

SYSTEM CHARTER

A description of the responsibilities of the system.

SYSTEM FUNCTION STATEMENT

A list of the use cases that must be supported to meet the system requirements.

Chapter 3

Domain Analysis: Defining Classes

■

Identifying Key Classes

■

Identifying Key Abstractions in the Gymnastics System

■

Summary: Progress So Far

IDENTIFYING KEY CLASSES

THIS SECTION IDENTIFIES the candidate classes of the Gymnastics System.

The term *candidate* is used because the definitions of the abstractions that are important to this system are just starting. The definitions of these classes and objects will evolve as you get further into the analysis. In fact, it is a characteristic feature of the Booch method that the products of object-oriented analysis and design closely reflect your understanding of the system being modeled.

The goal of defining key classes is to identify major abstractions in the problem domain. These will serve as main points of discovery about how the domain works and what data it contains. This means that the focus must be on the problem domain itself, concentrating on the logical things that will be part of the solution domain regardless of the system-development effort under way.

For example, if the system were to have payrolls, there would be employees and taxes, regardless of whether payroll were done by an automated system on modern computers or by a clerk with a lead pencil and an adding machine. Studying computers would not help you learn about payroll, but talking to a clerk probably would. Looking at a terminal would not help you understand payroll, unless the terminal was displaying a ledger.

Discovering Key Classes

Your first step is to underline the nouns. This is a quick trick that often helps when you are given a written problem statement. The technique can be useful because nouns often correspond to classes.

A few words of warning:

- The problem statement often includes implementation characteristics; you are interested only in logical classes at this point.

■ The problem statement may contain contextual information irrelevant to the system's responsibilities, and you
may not care about those classes.

■ Natural language is inherently ambiguous—there may be
aliases, or one term may be overloaded (apply to several
different things).

■ A given concept can be described using either noun or
verb phrases—for example, *shopper* or *someone shops.*

■ The nouns may be classes (team), but they may also be
objects (pommel-horse event), relationships, or attributes
of classes.

For all of these reasons, this parsing technique can produce
a great deal of noise. It can also be tedious to apply to large
problems. Nevertheless, it can be helpful in identifying the initial
candidate classes.

Once the initial candidate classes have been identified, the following analysis techniques can be used to filter the key classes:

■ Examine the tangible things and the roles they play in
the system.

■ Outline the steps necessary to complete the use cases
listed in the system function statement. Identify the
objects that participate in the scenario.

■ Identify the responsibilities of each class, the knowledge
the class maintains, and the actions it provides. List the
classes that collaborate with it to support these responsibilities.

Building a Data Dictionary
The data dictionary is a central repository for the abstractions that
are relevant to the domain. As candidate abstractions are discovered,
they are added to the dictionary.

Some of abstractions in the dictionary will turn out to be classes, some relationships, and others simply attributes of other abstractions. As analysis proceeds, the dictionary will be refined by adding new abstractions and removing irrelevant ones.

Maintaining a data dictionary helps establish a consistent vocabulary that can be used throughout the project.

Choosing Meaningful Names

Classes are named for the part of the domain they represent. A semantically meaningful name should be used for each class. A good name is simple and provides significant semantic information. It should be evocative—that is, the name should bring to mind the abstraction represented by the class.

Choose a name that

- Is a singular noun (unless the class represents a collection) or an adjective and a noun

- Best characterizes the abstraction (a person knowledgeable about the domain should be able to describe the abstraction at a high level based on the name alone)

The inability to name a class simply and clearly is a symptom of an ill-defined abstraction; it can be a warning sign of incompleteness, weak cohesion, and/or strong coupling.[1]

Cohesion refers to the strength of association of the member data and functions of a class; a good class has strong relationships among its operations—that is, the operations have a common set of inputs (class state or data) or outputs (for example, class-attribute values).

Coupling refers to the amount of dependency this class will have on other classes. A good class has loose, or weak, coupling; it does not have a lot of relationships to other classes outside of its supertypes or subtypes.

---

[1] Grady Booch, *Object-Oriented Analysis and Design with Applications* (Redwood City, CA: Benjamin/Cummings, 1993); see pp. 136–138 for a discussion of how these concepts from structured design also apply to object-oriented design.

Good names and definitions form the basis of clear communication for the problem domain. Clear communication is essential between analyst and customer, between analyst and designer, and among the project team members who will be implementing the system.

Staying at a Logical Level

Domain-related classes are logical or conceptual; they are independent of any given implementation of a system. They represent the "whats," not the "hows." If the Gymnastics System were to be implemented on computers, you might see, in the implementation, terminals and files. You should not see them in the key-abstractions view; this view should have no "footprints" of a previous or future implementation of a system. (This distinction is more difficult to make when the system being modeled is some form of system software, such as an operating system, where files are often part of the problem domain.) Also, avoid the introduction of implementation artifacts, such as linked lists. During analysis you are interested only in the problem domain, not in how domain entities map onto an implementation.

For example, if the problem description contained discussions of file structures, graphical user interfaces (GUIs), and so on, you would ignore those until you had found the key logical structures. If you needed to analyze the implementation classes, you would do so during the design phase in a separate model for that level of abstraction. A gymnastics-league model should use, not define, a GUI; conversely, a GUI should work for a lot more than a gymnastics-league model.

Remaining Within the System's Scope

Concentrate on classes that are relevant to the domain and are needed to carry out the responsibilities listed in the system charter. For example, the problem statement could have gone on at length on the choosing of a site for a meet. That would lead to classes dealing with site characteristics and locations. Those are abstractions, but not of this system. This system does not have that responsibility.

IDENTIFYING KEY ABSTRACTIONS
IN THE GYMNASTICS SYSTEM

KEY IS A relative term. It is used here to mean major—that is, those items that will reveal the most about the domain. There is no true measure of how important something is, and there is no major harm in adding less consequential classes unless they distract the analyst from the major issues.

Finding Classes from the Problem Statement

What follows is a list of the significant words in the description found in the problem statement in Chapter 2.

The description is analyzed, paragraph by paragraph, looking for possible classes. Knowledge of the system charter and functions will help clarify which abstractions are key to the domain.

> We are about to model a <u>gymnastics</u> scoring <u>system</u>. Our mission is to automate the <u>definition</u>, <u>registration</u>, <u>scoring</u>, and <u>record</u> <u>keeping</u> of a gymnastics <u>season</u>.

Gymnastics System is the entire system, not one object. The project is best named Gymnastics System.

Definition, registration, scoring, and *record keeping* are operations that this system will have to carry out. These are general functions, not classes. As general functions, they will use the data and operations of many different classes to carry out their responsibilities. Thus they serve better as high-level groupings to illustrate the overall general function.

A *season* is an abstraction. It will have data characteristics, and may contain other abstractions. It is therefore a good candidate class.

> Here is a quick description of a gymnastics <u>league</u> and one of their <u>contests</u>: A league is a group of <u>clubs</u> that compete against each other. Each <u>team</u> recruits <u>members</u> to participate in the contests.

League is a key abstraction. The league consists of the clubs, gymnasts, and judges who participate in gymnastics events. One of the key responsibilities of the system outlined in the charter is to track teams and their members.

Contests is a vague word. Certainly contest will be a key abstraction, but a bit farther down in the statement are several other terms that could be considered contests.

Club is an entity in the Gymnastics System. A club and its members will need to be tracked. At this stage, **team** appears to be a synonym for *club*. To clarify the role of club and team in the system, return to the system function statement and identify the use cases involved in this portion of the system. List each of the actions that must be taken to complete the use case.

Use case: Register a club in a meet

1. Register the club in the meet.

2. For every competition in the meet, register the club members that are participating in that competition.

Club, competition, and meet are collaborators in this scenario. When a club is registered for a meet, must it enter all the competitions? The answer is no. Must a club have the same set of gymnasts entered in all competitions within a meet? Categorically no, or you could not have men's and women's competitions. In fact, the club enters some subset of its members in a competition. This subset is a team. When a team is in a competition, must it enter all the events? The answer is yes. Must a team have the same set of gymnasts entered in each event within any competition? Yes. Clearly club and team are both abstractions in the Gymnastics System.

Member is a candidate for a class. What is a member? A member is a gymnast who belongs to a club or a team. Member is a relationship that a gymnast has with a club or a team. Not all gymnasts must be members of a club at all times, so gymnast is a better name for the class than member. Member should be added to the data dictionary.

A typical <u>meet</u> consists of several <u>contests</u> held in the course of one <u>day</u>. For example, there may be a women's all-around, a <u>women's individual</u>, a <u>men's all-around</u>, and so on. There may also be <u>junior</u> and <u>senior competitions</u>. When a team enters a meet, it enters all the competitions. For each <u>contest</u>, each team enters the same number of members, who must compete in all the parts of the competition.

Meet is a key abstraction: it is a grouping of **contests**. Later in the statement, a **contest** has **competitions**.

Now is the time when you would confer with the customer, domain expert, or end user to sort out the overloaded terms. Instead, you will examine the sample output sketched in requirements analysis (see Figure 3-1) to better understand the components of a meet.

Meet: Town Invitational
Competition: Women's Senior Team
Date: 12/3/92

| Club | Event Scores | | | |
	Beam	Vault	Bar	Floor
Flippers	41.5	40.3	44.6	43.7
Acrobats	42.2	38.5	41.0	40.6
Tumblers	37.3	39.8	42.3	41.3
Jugglers	36.8	41.0	37.4	39.6
Page 1				

Figure 3-1 Sample Output

It appears from this output that a meet has competitions, one of which, the Women's Senior Team, is being reported here. Within this competition is a collection of events. So the key abstractions are **meet, competition,** and **event,** avoiding the overloaded term *contest* completely.

Is **day** a key abstraction? No, it is a minor structure containing a single piece of information. Studying and learning more about day will not help you understand the Gymnastics System any better. Day is a data type associated with attributes of the Gymnastics System; add it to the data dictionary.

> Each competition is a series of <u>events</u> run on different
> <u>equipment</u>. For example, the women's competitions
> involve <u>balance beam</u>, <u>vault</u>, <u>high bar</u>, and <u>floor
> exercise</u>. All pieces of equipment are in operation at the
> same time; each team's competing gymnasts perform
> on one piece of equipment and then rotate to the next.

Here is confirmation that **event** is a class. Note the use of the singular; a collection of events is a competition.

Equipment is a candidate for a key abstraction. Review the system charter and function statement to find out if there are any data that should be kept or operations that should be implemented regarding equipment. Since there are no inventory responsibilities for mats and so on, there seems to be no need to track equipment or have it as an abstraction within this domain. You can therefore omit it from the key abstractions.

As seen on the sample output, **balance beam, vault,** and so on are instances of **event**. Although they may need to become subclasses later, now there is no clear indication that one type of event would be treated any differently than another. So they will not become subclasses yet.

> Each event has a <u>judging panel</u> assigned to it. These
> people are <u>qualified scorers</u> for this event. Each <u>judge</u>
> rates each <u>gymnast</u> on the event and reports the <u>score</u>
> to a <u>scorekeeper</u>. The scorekeeper throws out the high
> and low scores and averages the rest. This is the gym-
> nast's score for the event. The team score is the sum of
> all gymnast' scores.

A **judging panel** is a collection of judges assigned to judge an event. **Judge** is the class being collected and is a key abstraction. Judging panel is a relationship between event and judge that identifies the judges assigned to score the event. Add it to the data dictionary.

Scorer is a role that a judge plays in the system—judges score events. *Scorer* is a synonym for *judge*.

Score is an abstraction, but it is not key. It is a data type that can be used to describe a team score, gymnast's score, and so on. It should be added to the data dictionary.

Scorekeeper seems to be a key abstraction, but it is not. Scorekeepers are required to implement the existing system, but if the whole system is automated, scorekeepers are not required. They do not carry out any domain policy in their own right; they only transport data from place to place with no logical change in that data. Scorekeepers are processors, and, if the decision is to keep them employed when the system is implemented, they may show up in the design. But they are not key domain abstractions and should not show up on the model of key abstractions.

> Competition scores are the sum of the scores for each of the events. Meet scores are the sum of the competition scores, and so on. In addition to running the individual meets, the league prepares the schedule of meets for the season, ensures that qualified judges are assigned, registers teams and gymnasts, and publishes seasonal standings.

Are **competition scores** and **meet scores** key abstractions? No, they are attributes of competition and meet with type score. Score has already been added to the data dictionary.

What about a **schedule** of meets? A schedule is a collection of meets and a required output of the system; therefore, the underlying classes must contain the information to allow a schedule to be built. It may become a design class as its form is defined, but it is not a key abstraction for analysis. The same logic applies to **seasonal standings:** The information must be maintained by the underlying classes so that seasonal standings can be calculated, but in its own right, it is not a key abstraction of the system.

DEFINING KEY CLASSES IN RATIONAL ROSE
1. Create a new design for the Gymnastics System.
2. Place a class icon for each of the classes, labeled with the name.

The Resulting Key Classes

Figure 3-2 shows the resulting class diagram. This is not likely to be the final answer. The goal is to capture the major domain items of interest. The initial decisions on classes should be done swiftly and with a minimum of debate, because this is the first pass in a very iterative process. The inclusion of something minor is not wrong; it may well be addressed later. You are trying to get the exciting part down first. The exclusion of something major at this stage is not wrong; it will appear later on as you go deeper into the analysis process.

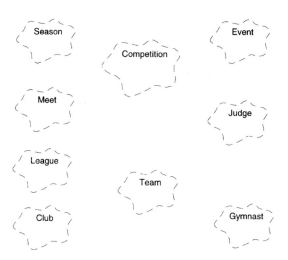

Figure 3-2 Key Classes of the Gymnastics System

Writing Class Specifications

Next, the semantics of the classes should be captured. A name alone, however good, is not enough.

A good definition is clear and concise. The description should include whatever is required to understand the concept or abstraction represented by the class. If necessary, include examples or point out what is *not* a possible instance of the class to aid in semantic distinction.

Describe the responsibilities of the class within the domain, and note any collaborators. This may lead to the discovery of new classes and relationships.

Add any restrictions and constraints that exist for objects of the class.

DEFINING CLASS SPECIFICATIONS IN RATIONAL ROSE

1. Double-click a class icon.
2. Fill in the documentation field of the class specification with a definition section and constraints.

Figure 3-3 shows some sample class specifications.

Class name:

    Season

Documentation:

Definition:

    A season is a time span in which teams of the league compete with each other.

Class name:

    Competition

Documentation:

Definition:

    A competition is a contest between two or more teams that is held at a meet. This contest will consist of several events.

Contraints:

    A competition must be part of a meet. There can be no more than one competition of the same type at any one meet.

Class name:

    Club

Documentation:

Definition:

    A club is a collection of gymnasts working as a unit in a league.

Figure 3-3 Sample Class Specifications

The Data Dictionary

The data dictionary shown in Figure 3-4 lists all domain entities that have been discovered so far. It is updated as analysis and design proceed. As the data dictionary grows it may become necessary to use a simple database to manage the information.

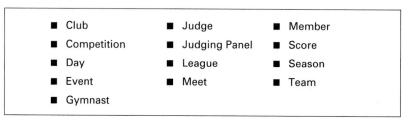

■ Club	■ Judge	■ Member
■ Competition	■ Judging Panel	■ Score
■ Day	■ League	■ Season
■ Event	■ Meet	■ Team
■ Gymnast		

Figure 3-4 Gymnastics System Data Dictionary

SUMMARY: PROGRESS SO FAR

AFTER COMPLETING THIS step, you have

- Discovered the major domain abstractions that will define the system

- Named the abstractions carefully and detailed their definitions to communicate precisely with all other system developers and customers

- Noted any rules or constraints that have been learned about the abstraction

- Built a data dictionary describing all the abstractions discovered so far

You have these deliverables:

- A class diagram containing only classes (see Figure 3-2)

- A class specification for each class containing the definition of that class (see Figure 3-3)

- A data dictionary describing all the classes discovered (see Figure 3-4)

Chapter 4

Domain Analysis: Relationships

■

Relationships

■

Refining Relationships

■

Defining Cardinality of Relationships

■

Summary: Progress So Far

■

Glossary

RELATIONSHIPS

CLASSES DO NOT exist in isolation. Rather they are related in a variety of ways to form the class structure of the domain. Relationships help further define the classes by exposing their content or dependency on the content of others. There are two key kinds of class relationships. The first of these is association, which denotes some semantic dependency among classes. The second is aggregation, which denotes a "part of" relationship.

Defining Associations

An association is a bidirectional relationship that occurs when there is a semantic dependency between two classes. For example, a judge scores an event, and an event is scored by a judge. This requires that Judge objects be aware of which events they judge, and that Event objects be aware of which judges they are judged by. This awareness is expressed by an association. In Figure 4-1, an association has been created between Event and Judge.

Figure 4-1 An Association Representing the Fact That Judges Judge Events

Although associations are bidirectional, they do not have to be implemented in both directions. If an association is traversed in only one direction, navigation can be restricted to that direction. During early domain analysis, it is sufficient just to recognize the association. As the model is refined, navigation paths are chosen for the association.

Defining Aggregations

Associations can be further specialized to form **aggregations** (some-times called has relationships). An aggregation represents a whole/part relationship, where the whole (also called the aggregate) contains or owns its part objects.

An aggregation occurs when

- An object is physically constructed from other objects (for example, an engine contains a cylinder)

- An object logically contains another object (for example, a shareholder owns a share)

An aggregation enforces exclusive ownership of the part object by its aggregate. For example a cylinder can be a part of only one engine, and a share can be held by only one shareholder.

In the Gymnastics System, an event is a part of a competition, and a competition is a part of a meet. Figure 4-2 shows these relationships.

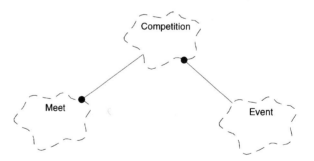

Figure 4-2 Aggregation in the Gymnastics System

Naming Relationships

Relationships must be given meaningful, concise names. A good name is simple and provides significant semantic information. The inability to name a relationship simply and clearly can be a warning sign of incompleteness or of several simpler relationships that were mistakenly gathered into one.

A relationship represents the ability to traverse from one class to another. Traversal of the relationship is from the source class to the target class. A relationship name often represents the role of the target class to the source. For example, the relationship `member` is traversed from `Club` to `Gymnast`. Member describes the role of `Gymnast` in relation to `Club` (see Figure 4-3).

Figure 4-3 Naming Relationships

Relationships in the Gymnastics System

Figure 4-4 shows relationships identified in the Gymnastics System based on the problem statement and sample output. Some of the relationships will be refined into aggregations as the domain is further analyzed.

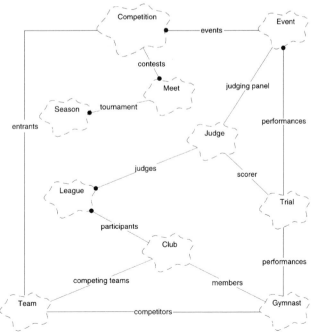

Figure 4-4 Initially Identified Relationships

ESTABLISHING RELATIONSHIPS IN RATIONAL ROSE
Add the associations and aggregations to the class diagram.
1. Choose the association or the has symbol from the icon palette.
2. Click the source class, and drag the mouse to the target class. Release the left mouse button.
3. Access the relationship specification by double-clicking the relationship icon.
4. Type the name of the relationship in the name field.
5. Click OK for the relationship specification.

Specifying the Meaning of Relationships

As with a class, a name alone is insufficient to define a relationship. In the documentation section of the relationship specification, you must add a definition for the relationship, as shown in Figure 4-5. Note that constraints are added to relationships, just as they were added to classes, if they apply.

Class Name:
    Meet
Public Interface:
Has-A Relationship:
    Competition contests
Definition:
    The contests that will be run at this meet.
Constraint:
    No two competitions of the same type can
    be held at the same meet.

Figure 4-5 Example of an Initial Relationship Specification

DEFINING RELATIONSHIP SPECIFICATIONS IN RATIONAL ROSE
1. Access the relationship specification by double-clicking the relationship icon.
2. Add the definition of the relationship to the documentation field.
3. Click OK for the relationship specification.

REFINING RELATIONSHIPS

WHEN IT IS difficult to define a relationship, further analysis often reveals new classes and relationships that need to be added. Figure 4-6 shows the judging panel relationship between Event and Judge. When it is examined more closely, several new relationships are to be introduced.

If it is difficult to define a relationship succinctly, you can write out a wordy description, such as "A judge judges an actual event at a meet." Is that "can judge" or "does judge"? He or she is qualified to judge any event of that type. Trying to define a single relationship between Judge and Event will be difficult—in fact, when you define these relationships, you will discover new classes.

These things are being represented with the judging panel relationship:

■ Judges must qualify to be able to score a type of event.

■ Judges are assigned to score an event at a competition.

■ Judges score a gymnast's trial in an event.

Figure 4-6 The Association `judging panel`

Discussing the different relationships will force a discussion of the different classes. One of the obstacles in the way of defining judges is determining what a judge is judging. There are three different "whats" here:

Event type is an abstraction of a possible Event that could be run at a meet. ***Balance beam***, in general, is an instance of event type.

Event is an abstraction representing the association of an event type with a specific competition. Balance beam, as part of the men's all-around being run today at 3 PM, is an instance of Event.

Trial is an abstraction representing the association of Gymnast with Event. Olga Korbut's performance on the balance beam in the women's all-around competition in the 1972 Summer Olympics is an example of a trial.

Once these classes are distinguished, it is easier to consider how Judge relates to each of these classes and to clarify the relationship, as illustrated in Figure 4-7.

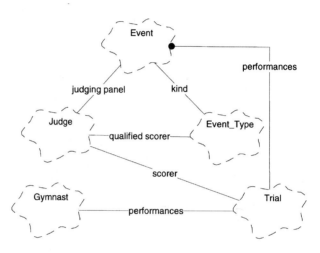

Figure 4-7 Refining the Judging Panel Association

DEFINING CARDINALITY OF RELATIONSHIPS

THE DEFINITIONS OF relationships to this point have left out any information on quantity. For example, a meet is likely to have more than one competition. The quantity of competitions at a meet is denoted by the cardinality of the relationship. Two pieces of information about a relationship are captured in its cardinality:

- Whether it is mandatory that an instance of the source contain an instance of the target (a meet must have at least one competition)

- The maximum number of target objects that can be contained by the source at any one time (a meet can have many competitions)

Figure 4-8 Illustrating Cardinality in a Class Diagram

Possible Cardinalities and Their Meanings

Figure 4-8 shows how cardinality can be illustrated in a class diagram. A simple notation is used to express cardinality. Table 4-1
shows which notation to use for each of the available combinations
of participation requirement and number of instances.

Cardinality Notation	Participation Requirement	Number of Instances
1	Mandatory	Exactly one
n	Optional	Zero or more
0..n	Optional	Zero or more
1..n	Mandatory	One or more
0..1	Optional	Zero or one
3..7	Mandatory	Specified range
1..3,7	Mandatory	Specified range or exact number

Table 4-1 Cardinality of Relationships

To determine cardinality, think always of any one instance of
the source class and then define

- Whether or not this instance must *always* participate in
  the relationship. If it must—that is, the relationship is
  mandatory—the lower bound will be 1; if the relationship is optional, the lower bound will be 0.

- The maximum number of instances of the target at any
  given time, given that there may be several instances of
  the target class for one instance of the source. This gives
  the upper bound.

Reflecting All States of a Relationship

Cardinality reflects the state of a relationship at any given time—that is, some relationships may have varying cardinality depending on the states of the objects involved. For example, when an event is actually being scored, it is mandatory that at least one judge be assigned. However, when you are first scheduling a meet, you do not know which judges will be assigned to an event, so you cannot force a mandatory relationship between event and judge. The cardinality of the relationship is 0..n. There will be a constraint mandating that judges be assigned when the event begins.

Saying it is mandatory that a meet have a competition means that you cannot define or create a meet unless you have at least one competition associated with it. If you remove all competitions associated with a given meet, you must remove the meet. It cannot exist without participating in its mandatory relationship.

The Cardinality of the Gymnastics System

Figure 4-9 is the updated class diagram showing the cardinality of the relationships.

Figure 4-9 Relationships with Cardinality

Define the cardinality of each relationship in the relationship specification. Include constraints that may restrict cardinality at certain times.

ADDING CARDINALITY IN RATIONAL ROSE
1. Access the relationship specification by double-clicking the relationship icon.
2. Add the cardinality to the cardinality to and cardinality from fields.
3. Add any constraints to the documentation field.
4. Click OK for the relationship specification.

SUMMARY: PROGRESS SO FAR

AFTER COMPLETING THIS step, you have

- Discovered major relationships between key abstractions

- Found additional abstractions based on analyzing those relationships

- Defined all relationships, including all cardinality and constraints, to further understand them and their meaning to the system

You have these deliverables:

- The class diagram with fully annotated relationships (see Figure 4-8)

- Class specifications for all abstractions, including the new ones found

- Relationship specifications for all the relationships (see Figure 4-5)

GLOSSARY

AGGREGATION

A whole/part relationship where the whole or aggregate is composed of one or more objects, each of which is considered a part of the aggregate.

ASSOCIATION

A relationship denoting a semantic connection between two classes.

CARDINALITY

The number of instances that participate in a class relationship.

Chapter 5

Domain Analysis: Defining Operations

■

General Approaches to Assigning Operations

■

Modeling Use Cases

■

Operations Required for Each Class

■

Summary: Progress So Far

GENERAL APPROACHES TO ASSIGNING OPERATIONS

IN GENERAL, THERE are two ways to assign operations:

- Define scenarios for each of the use cases in the system function statement and determine the operations that are needed to carry out those scenarios.

- Examine each class and determine what is required.

The operation usually should be assigned where the data or state resides that is needed to complete an operation.

Guidelines for Designing Operations

- Have each operation perform one simple function.

- Name each operation with a specific name that reflects the outcome of the function, not its steps.

- Avoid having too many inputs and outputs—this may indicate many functions that should be split into separate operations.

- Avoid input switches—they are often a sign of non-primitive functions.

Specifying Class Operations

Operations are added to the class specification, including any information that is known about the arguments. If the arguments are not apparent, they can be filled in later in design.

Operations that expose important characteristics of an abstraction should be indicated on the class diagram by their addition to cloud compartments.

SPECIFYING OPERATIONS IN RATIONAL ROSE

1. Access the class template of the class to which the operations will be assigned. Select < New > and name the diagram. Rose will bring up a clean palette with the object icons.
2. Choose < New > in operations. Rose will bring up an operations specification dialog box.
3. Enter the name of the operations. Enter arguments and results.
4. Rose treats the operations template separately from the class template. If you want to print the operations template, be sure to check the appropriate box on the print templates dialog box. A printout of the class template will simply list the operation names.

MODELING USE CASES

THE COMPLETE FUNCTIONALITY of the system is defined by the use cases listed in the system function statement. Expanding a use case into a detailed scenario shows the operations needed to realize the use case. Modeling scenarios shows which objects collaborate in the use case and identifies the operations needed in each object.

Using Object-Scenario Diagrams
Object-scenario diagrams describe how objects collaborate to realize a use case. They trace the execution of a scenario. The arcs of the object-scenario diagram represent messages passed between objects. They are labeled with the names of operations. Sequence numbers are added to show the relative ordering of the messages.

The object-scenario diagram is enhanced by the use of a script. The steps of the script align with the message invocations. The scripts express conditional statements and iteration.

Modeling a Scenario
The object scenario diagram in Figure 5-1 shows the operations in use when assigning a judge to the judging panel of an event. The numbers indicate a general sequence in which these operations will be invoked.

Assigning a judge to an event judging panel:

1. If the judge is not assigned already

2. and if the judge is qualified for this event

3. then add the judge to the event judging panel

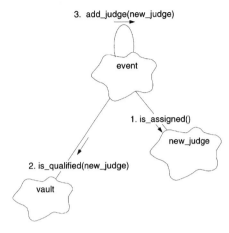

Figure 5-1 Scenario: Adding a New Judge to the Judging Panel for a Given Event

By stepping through the scenario, several new operations can be discovered. These are documented in the appropriate class specification. Developing object-scenario diagrams gives a more complete picture of the operations needed by each class.

CREATING OBJECT-SCENARIO DIAGRAMS IN RATIONAL ROSE

1. Select Browse from the menu, and choose Object Diagram.
2. Select <New> and name the diagram. Rose will bring up a clean palette with the object icons.
3. Place the objects on the diagram and label them.
4. Select the link icon, and place it between each pair of interacting objects by left-clicking the invoking object, dragging to the object with the message, and then releasing.
5. Select the message icon, and place it on each of the relationships.
6. To label the messages, double-click the message icon. Rose will bring up a message specification dialog box. List the operations in the operation box.
7. To specify the object, double-click the object icon. Enter the class name in the class box.

The "Uses" Relationship

Another way to show how a system will respond to a key scenario is on the class diagram with *"uses"* relationships (see Figure 5-2). This allows behavior to be demonstrated on a class diagram. The relationships must be labeled to show which operations are being used.

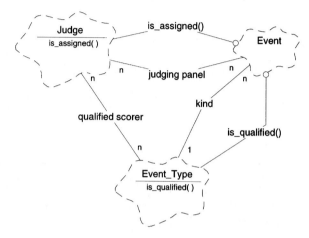

Figure 5-2 Class Diagram with "Uses" Relationships

A class specification will show which operations are present; this view highlights which class actually uses another and under which circumstances.

OPERATIONS REQUIRED FOR EACH CLASS

EACH CLASS CAN be considered individually to determine what operations are needed to complete the abstraction. The following steps are taken:

- List the roles and responsibilities of the class.

- Define the set of operations needed to satisfy these responsibilities.

- Ensure each operation is primitive.

- Add operations to ensure completeness. If in doubt about the suitability of a particular operation, it is better to sacrifice completeness for simplicity. The operations can be added later.

Listing the Operations for a Trial

The responsibilities of the class `Trial` are

- Record the score each judge gives the trial.

- Compute the overall score for the trial.

`Trial` must provide an operation that allows a judge's score to be recorded:

```
add_score()
```

The overall score of a trial (computed by dropping the highest and lowest scores and averaging the rest) is derived from each of scores the judges give the trial. `Trial` should provide an operation to compute the value of the overall score:

```
Score score()
```

Figure 5-3 shows the updated class specification for `Trial`.

```
Class name:
    Trial
Documentation
    Definition:
    A trial is the performance of a competing
    gymnast at a given event.

Operation name:
    add_score
Formal parameters:
    Score           score
    Judge           judge

Operation name:
    overall_score
Result:
    Score
```

Figure 5-3 The Class Specification for `Trial` *with Operations*

SUMMARY: PROGRESS SO FAR

AFTER COMPLETING THIS step, you have

- Determined the operations required to carry out the use cases in the system function statement
- Documented the needed inputs and outputs of those operations
- Assigned the operations to the appropriate class

You have these deliverables:

- Class diagrams showing operations (see Figure 5-4)
- Class diagrams showing "uses" relationships (see Figure 5-2)
- Class specifications updated to show operations (see Figure 5-3)
- Object-scenario diagrams showing key scenarios (see Figure 5-2)
- Object specifications

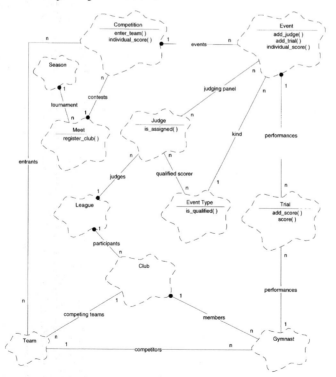

Figure 5-4 Class Diagram Showing Operations

Chapter 6

Domain Analysis: Attributes and Inheritance

■

Defining Attributes

■

General Approaches to Attribution

■

Assigning Attributes to Classes

■

Defining Inheritance

■

Identifying Superclasses

■

Identifying Subclasses

■

Summary: Progress So Far

■

Glossary

DEFINING ATTRIBUTES

UP TO THIS point, the discussion has concentrated on finding the major abstractions and the relationships between them. However, part of domain analysis is the location, definition, and assignment of less major, although still important, properties. The properties that describe a class are known as **attributes**. The process of finding them is attribution.

An attribute is equivalent to an aggregation association, where the label is the attribute name and the cardinality is exactly one. Figure 6-1 shows an attribute of class Gymnast.

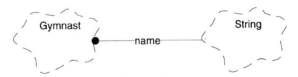

Figure 6-1 Gymnast with Attribute Name

Attributes can be shown on a class diagram in the cloud compartment. It is not necessary to show all the attributes in the cloud compartment, just those that represent key properties of the class. Figure 6-2 is an example of a cloud compartment.

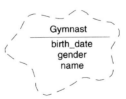

Figure 6-2 Cloud Compartment Showing Attributes

Attribute Types

A type is a class that represents the general nature of an attribute; attributes are instances of a type. For example, **birth_date** would be of type **date.**

Here are some characteristics of types:

- They are treated as synonymous with class in the Booch method.[1]

- They often represent small, reusable classes.

- They may be at a different level of abstraction than the domain—for example, more general.

Common classes that are used as types include

- Strings

- Addresses

- Dates

- Date ranges

- Time ranges

At a very low level of detail, attributes are often represented by base types of the implementation language, such as integer, character, and so on. Types are not explicitly modeled in diagrams as classes; however, they should be added to the data dictionary.

GENERAL APPROACHES TO ATTRIBUTION

THE TWO GENERAL approaches to attribution are

- Choose a class and list its properties, which are attributes.

- Choose a property from a sample output, input, or problem statement, and determine what it describes.

Both approaches are required for a complete set of attributes. Do not rely on all properties appearing in the problem statement or on your ability to identify all properties by thinking about a class.

---

[1]   See Booch, *op. cit.,* p. 65, for a discussion of the subtle differences.

Listing the Properties of a Gymnast

Among the attributes of a gymnast, you certainly will need to know his or her **name.** Since you must sometimes validate that a gymnast is permitted to enter a competition limited by age or gender, you will also need to know a gymnast's age and **gender.**

All of these are simple attributes that can be added to the class specification of gymnast. The important attributes can be shown in the cloud compartment.

One danger of just examining a class and listing properties is the ease of expanding beyond the system's requirements. There is no harm in some of this, because you want the class to be reused across many systems, but try to avoid an endless process of listing things that you could say about gymnasts. Hair color, eye color, and so on are all attributes, but they are not pertinent to this project. They should be omitted for now. They can be added later if they are needed.

Finding Attributes in Requirements Documents

Even if you have listed all relevant properties of classes first, you need to reinspect the requirements to ensure that you have not missed any attributes. If you find an attribute you have not yet specified, you need to define it carefully and try to determine which class it best describes. This may mean that you discover new classes; if so, you will create them, define them, and determine what relationships they have to other classes.

Unlike classes, relationships, and operations, where the nouns and verbs of the problem statement are a good guideline, attributes often are not mentioned in the problem statement. You have to use your growing knowledge of the domain and experience with the real world to identify them. Think of adjectives that can be used to describe an object; these often correspond to attribute values. Nouns followed by possessive phrases, such as "the name of the athlete" or "the time of the competition," are usually attributes.

Avoid any attributes needed only for implementation; you will get to them in the design phase. For example, a page number on a report is an attribute of a report abstraction, not the Gymnastics System.

Some attributes will be derivable from other information in the object and the environment; if these attributes are specified, they should be noted as derivable. For example, you can determine the score of the competition by totaling the scores for each of its events. You may choose to provide an operation to calculate the competition score when required rather than store it as a persistent data item.

ASSIGNING ATTRIBUTES TO CLASSES

MAKE SURE THAT the attribute describes only the class it belongs to— that is, you should be able to determine the value of the attribute based on knowing only which object it is of its class. If more than one object must be known, the attribute probably describes another related class.

Assume that it is a requirement, for historical reporting, to know what the full team roster is at any point in time. Gymnasts can change teams between meets. To be able to identify a team roster at a given time, you must keep track of the date a gymnast started and left a team.

To obtain the value of these dates, you would have to specify which gymnast and which teams. The attribute is not properly assigned to **Gymnast** or **Team** but to the relationship between Team and Gymnast. Therefore, you will need to convert this relationship into a class: **Membership. To** and **from** are attributes of **Membership.** Figure 6-3 shows the new class.

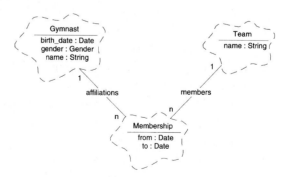

Figure 6-3   Discovering a Class During Attribution

DEFINING ATTRIBUTES IN RATIONAL ROSE

1. Access the class specification of the class that the attribute describes by double-clicking the class icon. Rose will bring up the class specification dialog box.
2. Click on the has relationship radio button. Choose < New > and double-click. Rose will bring up the relationship specification dialog box.
3. Enter the name of the attribute. Enter the type of the attribute in the class box. Click the radio control button for Public Access Control.
4. Click OK on the relationship and class specification dialog boxes.
5. Select the class on the class diagram.
6. Choose Compartment from the Edit menu. Select the attributes to be shown on the class diagram. Click the > > button, and click OK.

DEFINING INHERITANCE

MANY TIMES WHILE discovering classes, you might find yourself saying "This class is almost the same but different," or "This attribute applies to most of the instances of this class but not all of them." These are situations in which you may find that two classes characterize an instance: one class specific to the type and one that is more general. When you define a more general type, a **superclass**, and break it into specific subtypes, known as **subclasses,** you are modeling inheritance. Inheritance is that property of a class in which the class assumes all characteristics of its superclass but also takes on characteristics of its own.

The classic examples of super- and subtyping come from animal classification. Think of a superclass called birds and a subclass called penguins. A penguin is a bird and has a bird's characteristics for the most part, but it has some distinct qualities of its own.

Finding semantically correct inheritance structures provides good reuse, because the operations and attributes of the superclass do not have to be "reinvented" for each of the subclasses. It also allows simplification, because developers can work with the specific or general object as appropriate.

IDENTIFYING SUPERCLASSES

SUPERCLASSES CAN BE discovered by the realization that there is common data or behavior that describes a number of classes.

Assume that there is a need to mail programs and schedules to all people who may be involved in the league. It would be redundant to have separate mailing operations and attributes for judges, gymnasts, and so on. One person may be functioning in several of these roles but is actually a single physical entity. In this case, the requirement has indicated the need for **Attendee,** a more general class for anyone connected with a meet. Attendee's mailing address, name, and so on would be attributes of Attendee. See Figure 6.4.

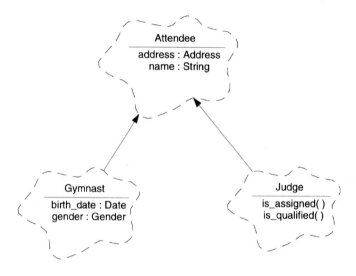

Figure 6-4 Discovered Superclass

Be careful not to confuse a reused type with an attribute that applies to more than one class. Types often apply to multiple classes. For example, there will be a date range associated with a season and a date range associated with a membership. There is no superclass of which membership and season are subclasses, however.

IDENTIFYING SUBCLASSES

APPLYING INHERITANCE CAN refine existing classes into specialized subclasses.

Sometimes it is useful to define subclasses of a class if certain attributes or operations apply only to a subset of the instances of a class. For example, if you had to compute the score differently for events with difficulty factors, you would need to have a different implementation of the method to compute the score. However, other operations are the same. You would prefer not to duplicate the common characteristics of an event, but you must do things differently for those objects that have difficulty factors. You can distinguish the subset as a separately described subclass—for example, vaulting event (see Figure 6-5).

If, however, the difficulty factor were just a piece of information that may or may not be of interest for any event, it would be an attribute whose value would not be required to be present. A subclass is not merited because there is no operational or semantic difference between those events with or without difficulty factors.

Sometimes there are subclasses but no real reason to distinguish them on the model. For example, there are different types of competitions: all-around, individual, and so on. However, if there is no difference in data content, operations, permitted relationships, or constraints, there is no reason to distinguish the subclasses.

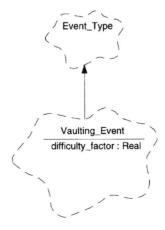

Figure 6-5 Discovered Subclass

DEFINING INHERITANCE IN RATIONAL ROSE

1. Choose the inheritance relationship and left-click on the subclass. Drag the relationship to the superclass and release.

2. Rose automatically notes the superclass in the class specification of the subclass.

SUMMARY: PROGRESS SO FAR

AFTER COMPLETING THIS step, you have

- Located most of the data attributes of the key abstractions

- Discovered and assigned the types of these attributes

- Discovered some additional key abstractions and relationships

- Discovered some relationships that will become classes because they have data attributes

- Found any subclasses and superclasses

You have these deliverables:

- An augmented class diagram that shows the inheritance structure, newly discovered classes and relationships, and cloud compartments showing important properties of the classes (see Figure 6-6)

- Class specifications for the new classes and relationships discovered

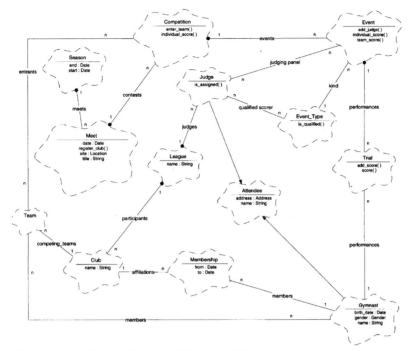

Figure 6-6 Class Diagram Showing Attributes and Inheritance

GLOSSARY

ATTRIBUTE

A property of a class represented as an aggregation relationship with a cardinality of one.

INHERITANCE

A relationship among classes, wherein one class shares the structure and behavior of another class

SUBCLASS

A class that inherits from one or more classes, which are called its superclasses

SUPERCLASS

The class from which another class inherits, which is called its subclass

Chapter 7

Domain Analysis: Validation and Iteration

■

Validating the Model

■

Iterating

■

Summary: Iterating Through the Cycle

VALIDATING THE MODEL

TO VALIDATE THE model, you check that the abstractions, operations, and relationships are sufficient to allow you to implement a system that satisfies the charter statement, which resulted from the requirements analysis.

Validating by Using Object-Scenario Diagrams

One method of validation is to pick one or more key use cases of the system (for example, computing the scores for a particular competition) and walk through each path, noting all operations that need to be performed. This can quickly reveal any missing classes, attributes, relationships, or operations.

As you saw in Chapter 5, you can use object-scenario diagrams, which show the set of operations that may occur in response to a given scenario.

Figure 7-1 shows the messages that are sent to determine a gymnast's score for a competition.

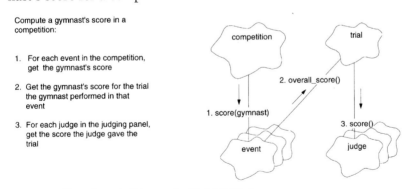

Compute a gymnast's score in a competition:

1. For each event in the competition, get the gymnast's score

2. Get the gymnast's score for the trial the gymnast performed in that event

3. For each judge in the judging panel, get the score the judge gave the trial

Figure 7-1 Object-Scenario Diagram for Model Validation

The object-scenario diagram illustrates the messages that are sent to determine a gymnast's score for a competition. You must verify that all operations are present and that there is a path from a competition to its events and from an event to its trials.

The overall score of a trial is computed from the scores that each judge gives the trial. Score is really an attribute of the relationship between Trial and Judge. This points out the need for an additional abstraction, **Raw Score.** Figure 7-2 shows the required update to the class diagram.

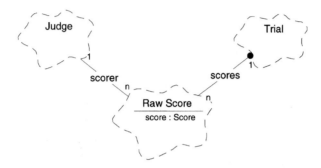

Figure 7-2 Updates to the Class Diagram

Figure 7-3 shows the corrected object-scenario diagram.

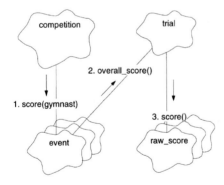

Compute a gymnast's score in a competition:

1. For each event in the competition, get the gymnast's score

2. Get the gymnast's score for the trial the gymnast performed in that event

3. For each judge in the judging panel, get the score the judge gave the trial

Figure 7-3 Object-Scenario Diagram for Computing a Gymnast's Score in a Competition

Validating by Checking Key Outputs

Another way to provide validation for the model is to match the model against key sample outputs (see Figure 7-4). There must be a way to obtain each piece of data; either it is an attribute with an associated operation to allow access to it, or it is a calculated field with an associated operation to return the value of the field.

Meet: Town Invitational
Competition: Women's Senior Team
Date: 12/3/92

	Event Scores			
Club	**Beam**	**Vault**	**Bar**	**Floor**
Flippers	41.5	40.3	44.6	43.7
Acrobats	42.2	38.5	41.0	40.6
Tumblers	37.3	39.8	42.3	41.3
Jugglers	36.8	41.0	37.4	39.6
Page 1				

Figure 7-4 Test Output

You need to examine each of the fields of this report and ensure there is an equivalent operation defined in the specifications. When this was done after the first draft of the operations, all fields were found except one: the team score for an event. Operations had been allowed for a gymnast's score for an event and a team's score for a competition, but not the team score for an event. This operation was added to event:

```
score team_score(team Team);
```

ITERATING

IN PRACTICE, OBJECT-ORIENTED analysis is not as rigidly ordered as it has been shown in this book. Once you are experienced, you can combine several steps at once. The order of steps can be interchanged when appropriate, and you will probably iterate through these steps several times before analysis is complete.

The Waterfall Model Meets Reality

If you are an experienced software engineer or a well-educated novice, you have some knowledge of or experience with the waterfall model of software development. This model dictates a strict, one-way progression from requirements specification to the finished implementation, each phase resulting in products that are handed off to the next phase and supposedly not altered afterward.

But the reality is that people seldom develop software like that, except when the problem is very small and constrained or the software project team has built almost identical systems before. Experiments in which professional software developers have been videotaped have concluded that

> software design appears to be a collection of inter-leaved, iterative, loosely ordered processes under opportunistic control.... Top-down balanced development appears to be a special case occurring when a relevant design schema is available or the problem is small.... Good designers work at multiple levels of abstraction and detail simultaneously.[1]

Many people find that creativity cannot be forced by creating a set of rules and required products, and an insistence on following the waterfall can result in wasting a great deal of energy trying to update frozen specifications when implementation results in necessary design changes. When dealing with a complex system of a sort you have not worked on before, you may find—like most developers—that you will naturally tend to adopt an approach that Booch has found to be a good match for object-oriented analysis and design, which has been called round-trip gestalt design.[2]

---

[1] B. Curtis,...*But You Have to Understand, This Isn't the Way We Develop Software at Our Company*, MCC Technical Report Number STP-203-89, May 17, 1989 (Austin, TX: Microelectronics and Computer Technology Corporation). As quoted in Booch, *op. cit.*, p. 189.

[2] M. Druke, private communication quoted in Booch, *op. cit.*, p. 188.

Round-Trip Gestalt Design

"When faced with a problem you do not understand, do any part of it you do understand, then look at it again."[1]

This is the essence of the approach to creating software recommended here. Round-trip gestalt design is incremental and iterative. It encourages you to make a quick model of the system, analyze it, and then refine it based on your ever-increasing understanding of the problem. Keep iterating this process until you are satisfied with the completeness and correctness of your analysis.

If you are managing a software project, you might feel a bit uneasy with this approach. However, it is not as unstructured or freewheeling as you might fear. Look at the process as an orderly spiral staircase, where each circuit results in additional progress forward and upward.

How Do You Start? When Do You Stop?

How to start has already been described: by learning the vocabulary of the problem domain and identifying the key abstractions. But given the "fuzzy," incremental, iterative process described here, how do you know when you are through?

At any given stage in the development of a prototype, analysis can stop and design can begin when the following goals have been accomplished:

- You have identified all domain entities that will play a role and defined their classes.

- You have specified the relationships between each of these classes.

- You have associated with each class all operations performed by or on it.

- You have analyzed each operation to the point where you understand what it needs to do and what other classes are involved.

---

[1] R. Heinlein, *The Moon Is a Harsh Mistress* (New York: Berkeley Publishing Group, 1966), p. 290. As quoted in Booch, *op. cit.*, p. 189.

In other words, when you have iterated through the analysis and walked through all key scenarios, and you have discovered no new classes, relationships, or operations, then analysis is complete.

At this point in this book, only a first pass has been taken through domain analysis; it is not complete. However, it is complete enough to move on to design; in that process, you are likely to return to find some new classes and access paths.

SUMMARY: ITERATING THROUGH THE CYCLE

IN THE PRECEDING chapters, a series of steps has been followed in domain analysis. Despite the sequential list, the reality of analysis is to move back and forth through these steps a number of times until the final result has been achieved.

When you have completed domain analysis, you have

- Identified all of the key abstractions and the relationships between them

- Identified all the needed attributes and operations to carry out the system's charter

You have these deliverables:

- A complete class diagram (see Figure 7-5)

- Class specifications for all classes defining the class, its relationships, its attributes, its superclasses, and the interface of its operations

- Object-scenario diagrams showing the use of operations in the use cases of the system

- Object specifications tying the objects to their classes

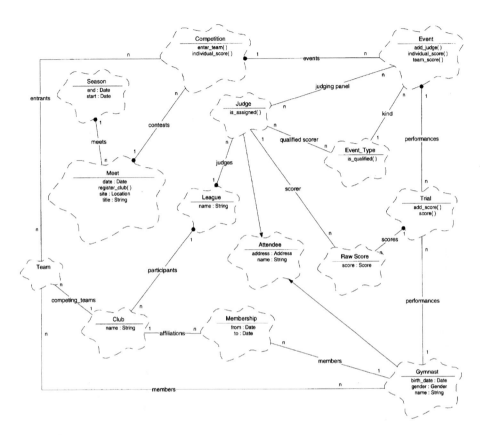

Figure 7-5 Complete Class Diagram

Chapter 8

System Design: Overview

■

Definition of Design

■

Principles of Design

■

Steps of Design

■

Products of Design

■

Glossary

DEFINITION OF DESIGN

ANALYSIS FOCUSES ON understanding the domain; in design, the focus is on how the domain requirements can be implemented.

System design is the process of expanding what was learned during domain analysis into a working implementation. Design is a series of decisions on what is the most cost-effective implementation that will carry out the system charter and lead to reuse among many systems.

There is no cookbook method that can tell you all the steps involved in creating a good design. Therefore, this chapter and those directly following it offer general advice and broadly describe the types of activities involved in design.

PRINCIPLES OF DESIGN

The following sections describe some basic principles of sound software design that will be applied in this chapter, as well as Chapters 9 and 10.

The Importance of Architecture

Most software systems have an extended life in which they will be worked on by a succession of development teams, ported to new software or hardware, and reworked to support new requirements. A system with a clean, well-organized internal structure, or **architecture,** will be easy to understand, test, maintain, and extend.

A good architecture is typically organized in layers. Each layer provides the basis of implementation for the layers above it. Communication is a one-way process: A layer uses the services of the layers below it but has no knowledge of the layers above it.

The lower layers of the architecture provide logical interfaces to system-dependent hardware and software services. This allows the system to be ported to other platforms by rewriting a single layer.

Layers are divided into loosely coupled partitions, each providing one kind of service. In the Booch method, these partitions are called **class categories.** Each category provides a group of related services that are meaningful at that level of abstraction.

Class categories provide well-defined interfaces to the rest of the system. The class-category interface specifies the set of functionality that the class category supports but does not specify how the class category is implemented internally. This allows each class category to be designed and implemented independently. As the system evolves, the implementations can be changed without affecting the rest of the system.

Separating Domain and Implementation

Strive to keep the logical and physical aspects of a system independent of each other. During system design, the only changes you make to the domain portion of the system (which was studied and documented during analysis) should be those due to the discovery of new aspects and further detail of the domain itself. This separation will allow the domain portions to be more easily maintained, since the maintenance programmer will not have to deal with the complexities of the implementation. The domain portions will be reusable across more than one implementation, such as for a product that will be released on a variety of platforms or with different GUIs.

You should also attempt to keep the implementation structures of the design free of the domain specifics of the system. Ideally, you should be able to reuse classes required for a good GUI, for example, across many different domains.

To achieve this independence, you will be building classes whose primary goal is to map between the domain and a chosen architecture for the system. The design will be organized into class categories that will encapsulate the details of the domain apart from the details of the design but allow some visibility and interface between the two to allow for a working implementation.

Taking a Progressive, Iterative Approach

One of the advantages of object-oriented analysis and design (as compared to previous methodologies) is that, during design, there is no need to create a model that is different from the one created during analysis. The basic object-oriented paradigm serves equally well in modeling the real-world requirements and the software implementation.

About three times more detail is required for a working implementation than for the domain analysis. A more progressive approach to design, an iterative approach rather than a full-scale leap, is now even more imperative than it was during domain analysis. Trying to do all the design in one step is far too complex to lead to good quality or even a working system.

To achieve a series of smaller steps, successive executable releases are defined that will eventually be integrated into a full-scale system. Each executable release is a piece of a system built to test or expose the design of a specific area. It is implemented, tested, revised, and then refined to fit into the final model.

Iterative development allows users to see working versions of the software earlier. User feedback generates new requirements. Because these new requirements are discovered early, the system can be adapted to satisfy them.

The development schedule is based on the shorter development cycles of each executable release, making it easier to estimate and track, and providing greater control and predictability over the lifecycle. Problems can be identified and corrected early, without jeopardizing the schedule.

System integration occurs during the lifecycle, eliminating the more risky "big bang" integration that often occurs late in the lifecycle. Testing and documentation also can be done iteratively, in parallel with the design of the system.

Designing for Reuse

Possible levels of reuse form a hierarchy. The higher the form of reuse is in the hierarchy, the more significant is its benefit. The lowest level of reuse is abstraction reuse, and the highest is architectural reuse. Reuse provides the major payoff of object-oriented design.

Designing for reuse began in domain analysis, when the time was taken to define the classes of the domain to fit any system using that piece of the enterprise. This is an example of abstraction reuse.

The careful separation of the implementation from the domain adds to the likelihood of good reusable classes. When designing the implementation, you need to continue to think about the world as a whole, while concentrating on this system's needs, to produce a set of implementation classes that can be used over and over again.

During design, two other levels of reuse will be identified: mechanism reuse and architectural reuse.

Mechanism reuse is the reuse of collaborating collections of objects that provide a particular function. An example of a reusable mechanism might be the collection of classes and objects necessary to allow a user to scroll and select from a menu of choices.

As the semantics and implementation of the classes are identified, the designers should be aware of patterns of behavior, which represent opportunities for mechanism reuse.

Architectural reuse is where entire layers of the architecture are reused across systems. Examples of reusable architectures are Motif^{TM} and OPEN LOOK^{TM}.

STEPS OF DESIGN

AS IN DOMAIN analysis, there is not one "firm" sequence for doing a design. The following are the steps used in this case study, but, as always, they are guidelines rather than rigid procedures for developing the products of design:

- Define the initial architecture.

- Plan executable releases.

- Develop executable releases.

Although not mentioned as a specific step in design, object-oriented design is also an iterative process of incrementally adding more detail. The design may highlight inconsistencies in the analysis model and make it necessary to iterate through analysis one more time. In fact, don't be surprised if you find yourself iterating through analysis and design several times before you are through.

Defining the Initial Architecture

Defining the initial architecture is a key step in design, one that may have far-reaching consequences in terms of the future maintainability and extensibility of the system. Because the architecture is fundamental to producing and maintaining many releases of the system, it is important to look beyond the first release of the system when designing the initial architecture.

Nevertheless, it is essential to maintain a balance between overemphasizing future maintainability and extensibility requirements of the system and under-defining the structure of the architecture. The former often results in delayed schedules, and systems that do not provide acceptable performance because they are so resource intensive. The latter results in systems that, over time, become extremely difficult to maintain and extend.

Planning Executable Releases

Do not try to design and implement an entire system in one large leap. The magnitude of the task is too large and the complexities too deep to allow the careful examination and testing required for a quality system.

Rather, build a system in a series of identifiable groups of related functions and tasks, or executable releases.

A executable release is a "mini-system" with a predefined goal. It is usually a combination of

- New, actual code that will be used in the completed system

- Completed, working code that has been through an executable release and tested

- Artificial utilities, dummy databases, or other artifacts quickly developed to allow an executable release to be verified or operate without having to build the complete design

- Simplified implementations of new classes, such as
  simpler standard data types substituting for what
  will become a defined data type

Part of setting up a good design plan is to identify potential
executable releases and their needs. You must also set up an incremental plan to build the system using successive executable releases
that you will eventually integrate to provide a complete system.
Integration will include completion of missing parts, replacement
of artifacts, and replacement of simplified data types with more
rigorously defined types.

The heuristic for planning the order of releases is based on
reducing development risk. Each executable release is used to elimi-
nate some risk in the project. This approach allows testing of the
key aspects of the system early in the lifecycle. Knowledge gained
from the early releases may change the priorities for subsequent
releases.

Key risk areas are areas anywhere in the system's design or
requirements that are possibly incomplete or incorrect.

There may be an area where the customer is uncertain what
the real requirements are; the customer will need to "play" with a
system to see if what was asked for is what is really wanted.

It may not be clear which is the most effective user interface.
In this situation, a release that can be tried out on prospective
customers will help determine screen layouts, fonts, and so on.

New services, hardware, or other systems may be untried; until
they are tried, it is unclear how to best utilize them in the design.

For example, an object-oriented database has been chosen for
the Gymnastics System. One concern might be how well this relatively new technology can be used. The vendor package may have
bugs or unclear documentation. There may be a long learning curve
in discovering how to use the database effectively. There may be
a conflict in using the database schema or utilities in the chosen
programming environment, operating system, or programming
language.

If you try to implement all the persistent data at once on this database, major redesign or fault counts may occur. If instead you focus on one part of the system that uses the database heavily and learn what faults occur there, assess learning times, and determine needed redesigns, it may be possible to avoid these problems with the rest of the system and significantly reduce the overall project-development time.

Testing occurs during each release, ensuring that the goals of the release were met. In this way a set of test suites is built up incrementally. These test suites form the basis of regression tests in later releases of the system.

Executable Release: Scoring Report

Goal:
> Verification and successful use of navigational paths and score derivation logic for the scores of a competition.

Classes to be implemented:
> Competition, Event, Trial, Raw_Score, Team, and relationships between them.

Previously implemented classes to use:
> Team

Use cases to be implemented:
> Determining the score of a trial
> Determining the results of an event (teams only)
> Determining the results of a competition (teams only)

Inputs:
> Dummy database (validated in advance) with a meet, a competition, all events for that competition, all competing teams and gymnasts for the competition, and all trials and raw scores.

Ouputs:
> The data needed to build the report on Figure 10-2, "Output of the Gymnastics System.
> A DB utility dump of the raw input for comparison.

Figure 8-1 A Plan for an Executable Release

An executable release plan will contain

- The goal of the executable release

- The classes (or portions thereof) that will be
  implemented in this executable release

- The use cases to be implemented

- Required inputs and input simulations

- Required outputs and output simulations

Figure 8-1 on page 91 shows an example of an executable
release plan.

Developing Executable Releases

Executable releases are built to demonstrate capabilities of the
system. Here are some major reasons for developing an executable
release:

- Demonstration that a system can work in a high-risk area

- Demonstration that a system can carry out a key
  mechanism

- Making some functionality available to users early in the
  lifecycle to obtain feedback

Developing an executable release involves the design and implementation of classes, the addition of new classes, and the detailed
specification of operations.

The executable release shown in Figure 8-2 is defined for the
Gymnastics System.

Executable Release: DB Test

Goal:
Verification and successful use of the Tupelo DataBase Manager

Classes to be implemented:
Team, Gymnast, Member with custodial operations and all attributes. No relationships with other classes than these will be implemented.

Use cases to be implemented:
Creating a team
Changing team members

Inputs:
Team, member, and gymnast creation test scenarios

Ouputs:
A database dump showing the successful storage of all required attributes and relationships. A database query using Tupelo utilities showing teams and their members with all attributes.

Figure 8-2 An Executable Release for the Gymnastics System

PRODUCTS OF DESIGN

UPON COMPLETION OF design, you will have

- *A class-category diagram,* which is a specialized class diagram that shows the chosen categories, or high-level organizational structures, and their visibility to each other. The class-category diagram represents the architecture of the system.

- *Design class diagrams,* which show the implementation classes. These will include diagrams that focus specifically on implementation categories, such as the key abstractions of a GUI, and diagrams that show the mapping of the domain to the design, such as a view of a domain class interfacing with data structures to allow an implementation.

- *Completed class specifications,* which show implementation and complete domain detail, such as the algorithms to use to carry out the operation, data attributes needed for internal operation use, and access control over operations and data to show which members are available to other classes.

- *Design object-scenario diagrams,* which show the full implementation detail of a key mechanism, including those objects that deal with I/O, data structures, and persistent data.

- *Architectural descriptions.*

- *Executable release plans.*

GLOSSARY

ARCHITECTURE

The internal structure or organization of a system.

CLASS CATEGORY

A logical collection of classes that provide a set of services.

System Design: Initial Architecture

■

Defining an Architecture

■

Choosing Major Service Software

■

Defining Class Categories

■

Summary: Progress So Far

■

Glossary

DEFINING AN ARCHITECTURE

DEFINING THE INITIAL architecture includes making strategic decisions on services such as a GUI, persistent object storage, communications software, and so on.

The architecture also includes the partitioning of system classes into groups that will be encapsulated to allow parts of the system to be developed in detail without having to look at all of the system at one time.

CHOOSING MAJOR SERVICE SOFTWARE

ANY SOFTWARE SYSTEM needs service software to carry out the major implementation work. This software may include

- An operating system

- GUIs

- Database managers

- Device interfaces

- Other I/O mechanisms

- Multiprocessor interfaces

Whether these are built or bought, their interfaces and the ability to access these functions are a major portion of the design.

The topic of how to choose these services is beyond the scope of this book. However, because these services affect the entire design and will have a major influence on design choices, the high-level decisions must be made early in the design process. Knowledge of the overall functionality of these services and how, at least on a high level, the remainder of the system will interface with them is an initial decision of design that should be made before getting into more implementation detail.

This does not mean that this part of the architecture will be static for the rest of the design; as detail is worked out, you may decide to choose different services, increase or redo their functionality, or change their interfaces. This step provides a starting point, however, for the remainder of the design decisions.

For the Gymnastics System, you will use a simple GUI and a simple object-oriented database for persistent data. There is only one processor, and everything can be run synchronously with acceptable performance (that is, there are no concurrency requirements). Real design is rarely that easy, but choosing this simplicity allows focus on the Booch method rather than explanation of complex design decisions. Figure 9-1 is a description of the architectural services used in the Gymnastics System.

Architectural Services for the Gymnastics System
User interface:

    EZ Report Generator
    Warp Windows

Database:

    Tupelo OO Database

Figure 9-1 Architectural Services for the Gymnastics System

DEFINING CLASS CATEGORIES

WHEN YOU ADD all the implementation classes, systems become too large to be described by one class diagram. Class categories are used to decompose the system into high-level logical "chunks," both to increase the understandability of the system and to provide a basis for future work assignments in the programming team.

Later in the design phase, you will refine the architecture, specifying the category interfaces in more detail. You may also need to add more class categories.

Choosing the Categories

A class category encapsulates classes, similar to how a class encapsulates interfaces—that is, users of things in a class category do not have to be exposed to all the classes in that category, just those that they will need to interface to the mechanisms that have been placed in that category.

Class categories also provide a "filing system" for developers. To be able to reuse something, you must first be able to find it. A large system can easily have more than a thousand classes, and a full enterprise can have lots of systems, so you need a way to locate existing classes rapidly. Certainly a CASE tool with a good browser helps, but, like any filing system, it will be effective only if good indexes are created. So part of choosing class categories is choosing strong logical groupings whose names are good indicators of where to find something. For example, to look for something dealing with gymnastics, you would go to the gymnastics class category; to find a certain data structure, you would go to the data structure category; to manipulate a window, you would go to the GUI.

Class categories are grouped around major architectural functions. Typically, the major groupings of class categories include the different high-level architectural structures, such as the database, the GUI, data-structure libraries, and so on. One category exists for the domain and systems control that will hold the system itself. If the domain is very large, it can also be broken up into more than one class category.

For the Gymnastics System, the following categories have been chosen:

- `Persistent_Data`, which provides database functionality

- `User_Interface`, which provides generic user interface capabilities

- `Data_Structures`, which is a class library of general data structures

- `Gymnastics_System`, which includes the domain

classes already defined and any additional classes
needed to implement them

- `Gymnastics_GUI`, which implements a GUI for the
  gymnastics system, using both the domain classes and
  the generic user interface capabilities provided by
  `User_Interface`

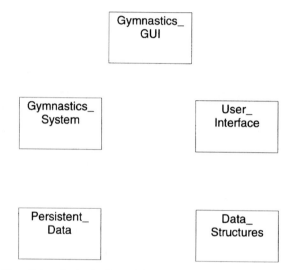

Figure 9-2 Class Categories in the Gymnastics System

Figure 9-2 shows a class-category diagram for the Gymnastics
System. Breaking the system up into the `Gymnastics_System` and
the `Gymnastics_GUI` allows for greater flexibility and extensibility. If the `Gymnastic_System` were to directly import classes from
the `User_Interface` category, the `Gymnastics_System` will be
tightly coupled to a particular user interface library. Modifying this
design so it can run with different windowing systems will require
modifying the `Gymnastics_System`. Moreover, a future requirement to make a number of different interfaces available would
require substantial rework to the `Gymnastics_System`. To aid in
future maintenance or possible porting of the system to different
platforms, this coupling should be reduced; that is, the domain
should remain unaware of the windowing system being used.

To achieve this, the class category `Gymnastics_GUI` is introduced. Its job is to tie the domain to a particular user interface system. If the system is ported to another user interface, this category will be replaced. However, if the domain structures are maintained independently of the user interface structures, the Gymnastics System itself will not be affected by the change.

If the system were larger, you could break the domain category into separate class categories that hold relatively independent portions of the system. For example, you may have chosen to separate the areas of the system dealing with meets, such as competition, meet, trial, and event, from that portion of the system dealing with members, such as judges and gymnasts. Because the system is tightly coupled, however, this is of limited use; one class category would end up using much of the other. A more classic decomposition might be one that separates a historical analysis and reporting structure from an operation structure. For example, in a payroll system, those classes in use for generating the payroll on a timely basis could be organized in one class category and those for analyzing tax reporting in another.

DEFINING CLASS CATEGORIES IN RATIONAL ROSE
1. Go to the top-level class diagram by choosing Top Level in the Browse menu.
2. Choose the class category icon from the palette, and place and name each category.

Defining Visibility
Visibility is the general term for exposure of the contents of one class category to another class category.

In a good design, some class categories do not need to see others; for example, there is no need for the `Data_Structures` to be aware of what `User_Interface` is being used.

There has to be some visibility, however; you could not define a working Gymnastics System without being aware of which data structures you choose to use or how persistent classes are represented. So the `Gymnastics_System` must use items in the

`Persistent_Data`. This is shown by drawing a "uses" relationship from the source, the `Gymnastics_System`, to the target, the `Persistent_Data`.

Some implementation class categories contain utilities and general data structures useful to any class category. These can be defined as global. The `Data_Structures`, which contains collection classes, might be used by any of the other categories.

Each class category will contain some classes that are available for use by other class categories and will probably also contain some classes that are never to be used outside the category. Classes that can be accessed by other categories are said to be **exported.** Classes for exclusive use by a category are local. This provides some encapsulation within class categories.

At this stage of the design, it may be too early to decide exactly which classes are available, but you can make an overall decision on whether any class within a category might be used by another. This is what you are documenting when showing visibility on a class-category diagram.

Later, as you detail the operations and learn what is needed to implement a needed function, you can specify in the class specification whether this class will be exported, and you can show the use of a class (an **import**) within another class category on a class diagram.

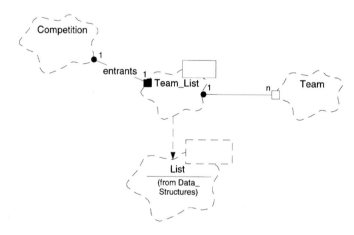

Figure 9-3 Importing Classes from a Class Category

Figure 9-3 is a class diagram in the `Gymnastics_System`. It will be built in Chapter 10. The parameterized class `Data_Structures::List` is defined in the class category `Data_Structures` and exported for use by this portion of the `Gymnastics_System`.

Figure 9-4 shows the visibility between the initial class categories in the Gymnastics System. The `Gymnastics_System` category uses (imports) classes found in the `Persistent_Data`. Another way to say this is that the `Persistent_Data` is visible to the `Gymnastics_System`. A "uses" relationship means that there is an interface between the two categories; it implies the ability to use classes from the target category. The category `Data_Structures` is global. All the other categories can use classes from this category.

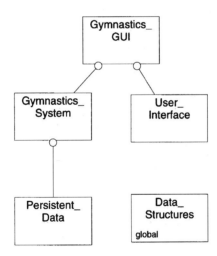

Figure 9-4 Visibility Between Categories of the Gymnastics System

The goal is to define class categories with a high degree of cohesion (that is, they are in the same area of the domain or they cover a similar set of implementation mechanisms and services) and weak coupling to other class categories (that is, only a small number of exports and imports cross category boundaries).

DEFINING VISIBILITY IN RATIONAL ROSE

1. Go to the top-level class diagram by choosing Top Level in the Browse menu.
2. Choose the uses relationship icon from the palette. Left-click the using class category, and drag to the class category that is being used.
3. For any global class categories, select the class category. Choose Specification from the Browse menu. Select global on the class category specification, and click OK.

Avoiding Rigidity

The class categories and the classes they contain are not rigidly defined. As you gain a better understanding of the problem and the relationships between categories during the design process, you can rearrange the categories and the classes within the categories to minimize coupling between categories.

SUMMARY: PROGRESS SO FAR

AFTER COMPLETING THESE steps, you have

- Determined the basic implementation services for use by the system

- Defined initial class categories for the domain and these services

You have these deliverables:

- A description of the architectural services of the system (Figure 9-1)

- A class-category diagram showing the categories to be used (Figure 9-2)

GLOSSARY

EXPORT

> When a class category makes a class available in its interface, that class is said to be exported.

IMPORT

> When a class category uses a class from another class category, that class is said to be imported.

VISIBILITY

> The ability of one class to see another and thus use its services. Classes are made visible to one another through export and import control in class categories.

Chapter 10

System Design: Developing an Executable Release

■

Building an Executable Release

■

The Steps of Design

■

Adding Control Classes

■

Detailing the Implementation of Operations

■

Adding Navigational Paths

■

Implementing Relationships

■

Defining Access Control

■

Summary: Developing an Executable Release

■

Glossary

BUILDING AN EXECUTABLE RELEASE

YOU PREVIOUSLY DEFINED the behavior of use cases during domain analysis and verified that analysis in the iteration and validation step. An even stronger validation can be obtained if you construct an executable release that implements the functions required in that use case.

The next step is to design the scoring executable release, which was defined in Chapter 8 (see Figure 10-1). It generates the content of the report shown in Figure 10-2 from a given input database. The executable release will be used to verify that the required paths, algorithms, and operations are in place to derive and generate this data.

Executable Release: Scoring Report

Goal:
 Verification and successful use of navigational paths and score derivation logic for the scores of a competition.

Classes to be implemented:
 Competition, Event, Trial, Raw_Score, Team, and relationships between them.

Previously implemented classes to use:
 Team

Use cases to be implemented:
 Determining the score of a trial.
 Determining the results of an event (teams only).
 Determining the results of a competition (teams only).

Inputs:
 Dummy database (validated in advance) with a meet, a competition, all events for that competition, all competing teams and gymnasts for the competition, and all trials and raw scores.

Ouputs:
 The data needed to build the report in Figure 10-2.
 A DB utility dump of the raw input for comparison.

Figure 10-1 Executable Release to Test Scoring

Meet: Town Invitational
Competition: Women's Senior Team
Date: 12/3/92

Club	Event Scores			
	Beam	**Vault**	**Bar**	**Floor**
Flippers	41.5	40.3	44.6	43.7
Acrobats	42.2	38.5	41.0	40.6
Tumblers	37.3	39.8	42.3	41.3
Jugglers	36.8	41.0	37.4	39.6
Page 1				

Figure 10-2 Output of the Gymnastics System

THE STEPS OF DESIGN

SYSTEM DESIGN FOCUSES on the lower-level details of the system. As executable releases are built, new classes that are not part of the analysis model but are needed for implementation are added. Domain analysis focuses on the client view of the system; system design focuses on how that view may be implemented.

Designing an executable release typically involves the following tasks:

- Adding control classes

- Defining new classes to support the implementation

- Defining operations needed to carry out the implementation

- Defining algorithms to implement the operations

- Providing implementations of the relationships in the analysis model

- Adding navigation paths

- Determining the necessary access control

There is no fixed order in which these tasks must be done. You will accomplish them as a natural consequence of building the executable release.

ADDING CONTROL CLASSES

MOST OF THE functionality of the system is placed in the domain classes. Some functionality involves a number of classes but does not naturally belong in any one of those classes. A typical example would be a sequence of operations that generates the result of some computation.

The designer could choose to spread operations that implement this behavior across a number of classes, but generally the solution will not be robust. A change in functionality could involve changes to many different classes. A better solution is to introduce a **control class.**

Control classes model functionality that is not naturally tied to any other class. They unite objects that collaborate to provide some behavior. Instances of the control class are often temporary and usually only last during the execution of the activity.

Building the report shown in Figure 10-2 involves the collaboration of the following classes: Meet, Competition, Event, Team, and Club. It is not clear which one of those classes should provide the operation to build the report. Rather than any one of these classes actually building the report, a control class, **Results_Generator,** is introduced. If the content of the report changes in the future, only the implementation of the Results_Generator will be affected. Figure 10-3 shows which classes Results_Generator uses to build the report.

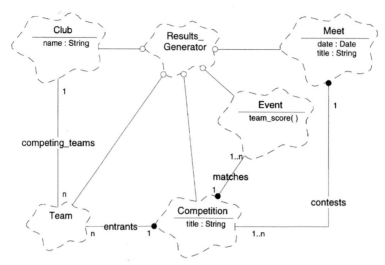

Figure 10-3 Class Diagram with a Control Class

DETAILING THE IMPLEMENTATION OF OPERATIONS

MANY OPERATIONS ARE simple enough that the specification in the domain analysis phase already provides an adequate description. Some operations do simple access of data in the object, update attributes, or update relationships. For example, the title operation in Meet simply returns the value of the attribute.

More complex operations, particularly those that involve interactions between many objects, need further definition. Results_Generator must provide an operation that collects the data for the competition report. An object-scenario diagram will expose the details of this operation.

Basically, the operation must find the data about the meet, locate each competing team, locate the events and their names, find the event score for each event and each team, and determine the competition score. The messages that must be sent to other objects are reflected in the object-scenario diagram shown in Figure 10-4.

Among the things to determine while developing this object-scenario diagram are

- Does each object have an existing defined class of which it is an instance?

- Is there a way for `Results_Generator` to locate each of these objects?

To allow `Results_Generator` to generate the report, it will need to be passed through the following input parameters: an object of class `Meet`, and an object of class `Competition`. All the other objects can be accessed through the `Competition` object.

Operations will be added to the classes to provide access to each of the attributes and relationships needed to build the report.

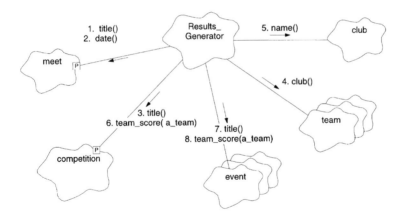

Building the results report for a competition:

1. Get the title of the meet

2. Get the date of the meet

3. Get the name of the competition

4. For each team in the competition get the team's club

5. Get the club's name

6. Get the team's overall score in the competition

7. For each event in the competition get the name of the event

8. For each team in the competition get the team's score in the event

Figure 10-4 Design of an Object-Scenario Diagram

Defining Algorithms

For some complex operations, an object-scenario diagram will not illustrate the detailed steps of the operation. An algorithm will provide a better definition of the real work involved.

On the object-scenario diagram in Figure 10-4, you see the nontrivial operation `team_score`. To compute a `team_score`, an `Event` will need to get the score of the `Trial` of each of the `Gymnasts` in the `Team`.

To provide that score, `Event` needs to find the `Trial` for that `Gymnast` and then compute the composite score from the `Raw_Scores`.

Consider the operation score that computes the net score of a trial. An object-scenario diagram reveals the steps of accessing each raw score but not the actual formula that must be applied to compute the net score. To show this formula, you need to provide a more textual statement of the logic of the operation

```
Score score( )
```

Determining this formula requires more detailed analysis. If this were a real system you were implementing, you could interview the scorekeeper to find out how scores are computed. In this case, the problem statement states the following:

> Each judge rates each gymnast on the event and reports the score to a scorekeeper. The scorekeeper throws out the high and low scores and averages the rest. This is the gymnast's score for the event.

These instructions can translate into a detailed algorithm for the operation score. A pseudocode could be used to define the algorithms for operations, but it is preferable to use the implementation language of choice at this stage (in this case, C++). Figure 10-5 shows the operation specification for the operation score. The algorithm has been added to the documentation section.

Examination of the algorithm reveals two things:

- The collection class `Raw_Score_List` will need to provide the minimum and maximum raw score.

- The ability to add raw scores is needed; that is, the Raw_Score class (as well as the score class) will need a + function.

```
Operation specification:
   Score net_score()
   {
       Score net_score = scores.first();
// Iterate over the scores and sum
       while !(scores.done())
       {
           net_score = net_score +
           scores.next();
       };
       // Throw out the low and high
       net_score = net_score -
       (scores.min() + scores.max());
       // Average by scores used
       net_score = net_score /
        (scores.length() - 2);
       return net_score;
   };
```

Figure 10-5 Adding Operation Detail to a Class Specification

DETAILING OPERATIONS IN RATIONAL ROSE

1. Double-click the class where the operation resides to access the class specification.
2. Choose the operation, and double-click to access the operation specification.
3. Add the algorithm and any comments in the documentation field.
4. If the operation has an associated object-scenario diagram, choose the appropriate object diagram from the object diagram list box.
5. Click OK for the operation specification. Click OK for the class specification.

ADDING NAVIGATIONAL PATHS

IN DOMAIN ANALYSIS, associations model semantic relationships between classes. Associations are inherently bidirectional, but some associations are traversed in only one direction. During design we begin to add navigation paths to the associations. This helps determine how the associations will be implemented. For instance, if an association is traversed in only one direction, it can be implemented as a pointer in C++.

Examine Figure 10-4 to determine the navigation paths needed for `Results_Generator` to build the report.

The association `competing_teams` between `Team` and `Club` must be traversed in the direction `Team` to `Club`. Add this information to the association specification.

IMPLEMENTING RELATIONSHIPS

Physical Containment

DURING DOMAIN ANALYSIS, a relationship signifies that objects of the related classes are somehow linked. In the design phase, we must decide how to implement the relationships. The implementation, or type of containment, can be specified in the following ways:

- *Containment by value:* contains an object

- *Containment by reference:* contains a pointer or a reference to an object

The choice of containment has implications for the lifetime semantics of the objects. Containment by value implies that the lifetime of the target object is equivalent to the lifetime of the source object. Construction and destruction of the target occur as a consequence of construction or destruction of the source. Containment by reference indicates that the lifetime of the target object is independent of the lifetime of the source object. Destruction of the source does not necessarily result in destruction of the target.

For example, a `Competition` physically contains its `Event` objects. If the `Competition` is cancelled, the `Events` will be cancelled also. On the other hand, a `League` contains a number of `Clubs`, but if the `League` is dissolved, the `Clubs` will continue to exist. Figure 10-6 gives examples of the different types of containment.

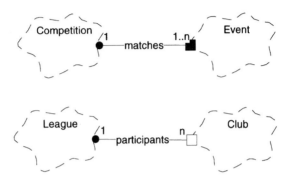

Figure 10-6 Specifying the Implementation of Relationships

SHOWING PHYSICAL CONTAINMENT IN RATIONAL ROSE
1. Double-click the relationship to be specified to access the relationship specification.
2. Choose the appropriate type of containment.
3. Click OK for the relationship specification.

In C++, containment by value is typically implemented by physically containing an object. Containment by reference is implemented by using a pointer or a reference. In pure object-oriented languages, such as Smalltalk, references are used to access all objects. In these languages, the implementor should ensure that the objects have the correct lifetime properties for the type of containment specified.

Adding Container Classes

Relationships of 0..n or 1..n cardinality require a container class to implement the relationship; the entrants relationship between Com-petition and Team is such a relationship.

Building container classes provides us with an opportunity to take advantage of reuse. Container classes make ideal **parameter-ized classes.** The type of the objects they contain is of little interest to the definer of the class. Therefore, they can be designed generally and instantiated again and again for particular implementations.

The container classes should be separated from the domain classes and placed in the Data_Structures category. Separating them in this way makes them independent of the Gymnastics System. Thus they will be available in the future for use in other systems. (Alternatively, a commercially available class library could be used.)

Create a List class in the Data_Structures category. To use List in the Gymnastics_System it must be imported from the Data_Structures category. The Team_List class is then **instan-tiated** from the List class, using Team as the actual parameter to be substituted for the formal type parameter in the List class. If shown on a design class diagram, it would look like Figure 10-7.

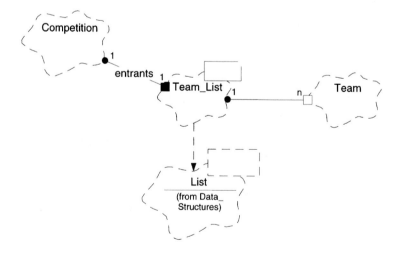

Figure 10-7 Implementation of Entrants

DEFINING ACCESS CONTROL

DURING DOMAIN ANALYSIS, limiting the visibility of or access to classes was not a concern; you could assume that every class had access to every other class's relationships and attributes, which helped in getting a global look at the problem and establishing that the key abstractions were complete.

The goal during the design phase is to be able to treat classes as "black boxes," where the implementation is completely hidden from the public interface. By encapsulating operations and attributes (also known as information hiding), dependencies on implementation are minimized and "fire walls" are created to contain the effects of change. This has the double benefit of localizing change so it is easier to understand and of allowing the implementation to change without requiring the clients of the changed class to be recompiled. Attributes and relationship embodiments (data members) are partitioned into types of access. Again, the specifications and class diagrams can show this directly.

Types of Access and Guidelines for Their Use
A member of a class can be

- *Public,* which means that any other class can address this operation or data member

- *Protected,* which means that only subclasses of this class can address this operation or data member

- *Private,* which means that no other class can address this operation or data member directly

- *An implementation,* which means that the class is declared in the body of an operation

In C++, it is possible to declare a class a friend of another class. If a class is declared as a friend, it is able to access all of the data members, including those marked private.

Here are some guidelines for limiting the scope of knowledge of an operation:

- Let each class perform operations on and provide access to information that it contains or that pertains to it. The operations can be left public while shielding the data.

- Always use an operation to access attributes belonging to another class, rather than directly looking at its data. Data members should remain protected or private.

- Operations that provide internal results of no use to other classes without additional information should remain private.

Add the access control to the relationship specifications, as shown in Figure 10-8. It will appear on the class diagram as an adornment on the relationship.

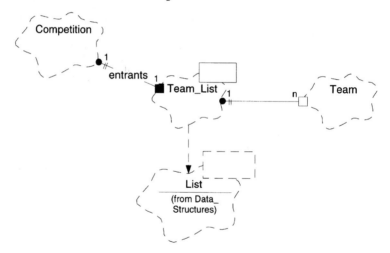

Figure 10-8 Class Diagram Showing Access Control

DETAILING ACCESS CONTROL IN RATIONAL ROSE
1. Double-click the class on the class diagram.
2. Double-click the relationship.
3. Select the appropriate type of access control.
4. Click OK for the relationship specification. Click OK for the class specification.

SUMMARY: DEVELOPING AN EXECUTABLE RELEASE

AFTER COMPLETING THESE steps, you have

- Added control classes

- Detailed the implementation of operations

- Determined navigational paths

- Specified the implementation of relationships

- Defined access control

You have these deliverables:

- Updated class diagrams showing the implementation of relationships, additional operations, and access control

- Updated class specifications showing operation specifications (see Figure 10-7)

- Design object-scenario diagrams for nontrivial operations (see Figure 10-4)

GLOSSARY

CONTAINMENT BY REFERENCE
Containing a pointer or a reference to an object.

CONTAINMENT BY VALUE
Physically containing an object.

CONTROL CLASS
A class that provides functionality that relies on the collaboration of a number of other classes but does not naturally belong in any of those classes.

INSTANTIATION

Producing a class by providing the actual parameters necessary to fill in the template of a parameterized class.

PARAMETERIZED CLASS

A class that provides some general-purpose functionality
and can be parameterized by other classes, objects, and/or
operations. Parameterized classes are typically used as
container classes.

PRIVATE

The portion of the interface of a class that is not visible to
any other class.

PROTECTED

The portion of the interface of a class that is visible only to
subclasses of that class.

PUBLIC

The portion of the interface of a class that is visible to all
other classes.

Appendix A

■

High-level Category Diagram

■

Analysis Model

■

Class Specifications

HIGH-LEVEL CATEGORY DIAGRAM

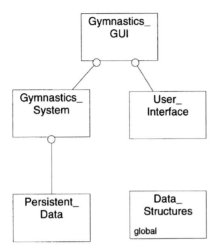

ANALYSIS MODEL

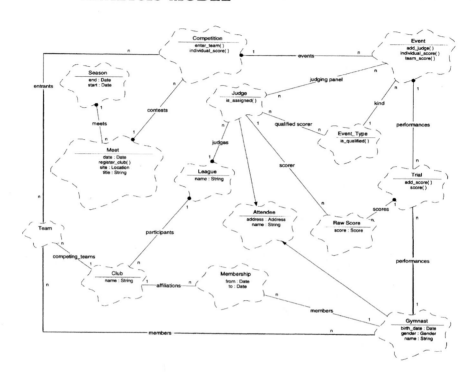

CLASS SPECIFICATIONS

Class Name: **Attendee**

Documentation:
Definition: An attendee is anyone who might or has attended a gymnastic meet.

Export Control: Public
Cardinality: n
Hierarchy:
Superclasses: none
Public Interface:
  Operations:
        name
        address
        work_phone
        home_phone
        set_name
        set_address
        set_work_phone
        set_home_phone

Protected Interface:
  Has-A Relationships:
        String   name
        Address   address
        Phone_No work_no
        Phone_No home_phone

State Machine: No
Concurrency: Sequential
Persistence: Transient

Operation Name:
  name

Public Member of: Attendee
Return Class: String
Concurrency: Sequential

Operation Name:
  address

Public Member of: Attendee
Return Class: Address
Concurrency: Sequential

Operation Name:
  work_phone

Public Member of: Attendee
Return Class: Phone_No
Concurrency: Sequential

Operation Name:
  home_phone

Public Member of: Attendee
Return Class: Phone_No
Concurrency: Sequential

Operation Name:
  set_name

Public Member of: Attendee
Return Class: void
Arguments:
            String   name
Concurrency: Sequential

Operation Name:
  set_address

Public Member of: Attendee
Return Class: Void
Arguments:
            Address   address
Concurrency: Sequential

Operation Name:
  set_work_phone

Public Member of: Attendee
Return Class: void

Arguments:
      Phone_No   work_phone
Concurrency: Sequential

Operation Name:
  set_home_phone

Public Member of: Attendee
Arguments:
      Phone_No   home_phone
Concurrency: Sequential

Class Name: **Club**

Documentation:
  Definition: A club is a collection of gymnasts
                         working as a unit in a league.

Export Control: Public
Cardinality: n
Hierarchy:
  Superclasses: none
Public Interface:
  Operations:
        add_member
        remove_member
        members
        is_member
        set_name

Private Interface:
  Has-A Relationships:
                         String   name

State Machine: No
Concurrency: Sequential
Persistence: Transient

Operation Name:
  add_member

Public Member of: Club
Arguments:
        Gymnast   member
        Date   date
Concurrency: Sequential

Operation Name:
  remove_member

Public Member of: Club
Arguments:
        Gymnast   member
Concurrency: Sequential

Operation Name:
  members

Public Member of: Club
Return Class: Gymnast_List
Concurrency: Sequential

Operation Name:
  is_member

Public Member of: Club
Arguments:
            Gymnast   member
Concurrency: Sequential

Operation Name:
  set_name

Public Member of: Club
Arguments:
            String   club_name
Concurrency: Sequential

Class Name: **Competition**

Documentation:
  Definition: A competition is a contest between
                         two or more teams that is held at a
                         meet. This contest will consist of several
                         events at which the same set of gym
                         nasts for each team competes in each
                         event.

  Constraint: A competition must be part of a meet.
                         There can be no more than one compe
                         tition of the same type at any one meet.

Export Control: Public
Cardinality: n
Hierarchy:
  Superclasses: none
Public Interface:
  Operations:
            enter_team
            individual_score
            team_score
            is_event
            events
            teams
            is_entered
            remove_entrant
            set_entrants
            add_entrant
            start_time
            set_start_time
            length
            set_length
            title
            set_title

Private Interface:
  Has-A Relationships:
                    Event   events
            Definition: A competition consists of a set of events
                        on different equipment, the total results
                        of which represent the competition
                        score.

Constraint: Each event in the competition
must be a different
Event_Type.

Time_Of_Day   start
               Minute   length
               String   title

Team_List entrants
Definition: A club enters a team in a competition.
Entrants represents all such teams
entered in a competition.

State Machine: No
Concurrency: Sequential
Persistence: Transient

Operation Name:
  enter_team

Public Member of: Competition
Arguments:
          Team   team
Concurrency: Sequential

Operation Name:
  individual_score

Public Member of: Competition
Return Class: Score
Arguments:
          Gymnast   gymnast
Documentation:
  Definition: Returns the score of the gymnast
represented by the argument gymnast.

Concurrency: Sequential

Operation Name:
  team_score

Public Member of: Competition
Return Class: Score
Arguments:
      Team   team
Concurrency: Sequential

Operation Name:
  is_event

Public Member of: Competition
Return Class: Boolean
Arguments:
      Event   event
Concurrency: Sequential

Operation Name:
  events

Public Member of: Competition
Return Class: Event_List
Concurrency: Sequential

Operation Name:
  teams

Public Member of: Competition
Return Class: Team_List
Concurrency: Sequential

Operation Name:
  is_entered

Public Member of: Competition
Return Class: Boolean
Arguments:
      Team   team
Concurrency: Sequential

Operation Name:
  remove_entrant

Public Member of: Competition
Return Class: Void
Arguments:
      Team   team
Concurrency: Sequential

Operation Name:
  set_entrants

Public Member of:	Competition
Return Class:	void
Arguments:	
Team_List	teams
Concurrency:	Sequential

Operation Name:
  add_entrant

Public Member of:	Competition
Return Class:	void
Arguments:	
Team	team
Concurrency:	Sequential

Operation Name:
  start_time

Public Member of:	Competition
Return Class:	Time_Of_Day
Concurrency:	Sequential

Operation Name:
  set_start_time

Public Member of:	Competition
Arguments:	
Time_Of_Day	start_time
Concurrency:	Sequential

Operation Name:
  length

Public Member of:	Competition
Return Class:	Minute
Concurrency:	Sequential

Operation Name:
  set_length

Public Member of:	Competition
Return Class:	void

Arguments:

        Minute   length

Concurrency: Sequential

Operation Name:
  title

Public Member of: Competition

Return Class: String

Concurrency: Sequential

Operation Name:
  set_title

Public Member of: Competition

Return Class: void

Arguments:

        String   title

Concurrency: Sequential

Class Name: **Date**

Documentation:
   Definition: Represents a date.

Export Control: Public
Cardinality: n
Hierarchy:
   Superclasses: none
Protected Interface:
   Has-A Relationships:
                String   day
                String   month
                String   year

State Machine: No
Concurrency: Sequential
Persistence: Transient

Class Name: **Event**

Documentation:
 Definition: An event is a specific contest within in a
               competition. It is of a particular event type.

Export Control: Public
Cardinality: n
Hierarchy:
  Superclasses: none
Public Uses:
                 Judge   is_assigned()

Public Interface:
 Operations:
                 add_judge
                 add_trial
                 team_score
                 individual_score
                 remove_judge
                 judging_panel
                 set_judging_panel
                 kind
                 Event
                 is_kind
                 Trials
                 set_trials

Private Interface:
 Has-A Relationships:
                 Trial   performances
                 Definition: The results of a gymnasts entry
                             in an event.

                 Constraint: An event must have a trial
                             for each gymnast who is a
                             competitor in the competition
                             of that event before the event
                             finishes.

          Time_Of_Day   time

State Machine: No
Concurrency: Sequential
Persistence: Transient

Operation Name:
  add_judge

Public Member of: Event
Arguments:
          Judge   judge
Concurrency: Sequential

Operation Name:
  add_trial

Public Member of: Event
Arguments:
          Trial   trial
Concurrency: Sequential

Operation Name:
  team_score

Public Member of: Event
Arguments:
          Team   team
Concurrency: Sequential

Operation Name:
  individual_score

Public Member of: Event
Arguments:
          Gymnast   gymnast
Concurrency: Sequential

Operation Name:
  remove_judge

Public Member of: Event
Return Class: void
Arguments:
          Judge   judge
Concurrency: Sequential

Operation Name:
  judging_panel

Public Member of: Event
Return Class: Judge_List
Concurrency: Sequential

Operation Name:
  set_judging_panel

Public Member of: Event
Return Class: void
Arguments:
          Judge_List   judges
Concurrency: Sequential

Operation Name:
  kind

Public Member of: Event
Return Class: Event_Type
Concurrency: Sequential

Operation Name:
  Event

Public Member of: Event
Arguments:
          Event_Type   kind
Concurrency: Sequential

Operation Name:
  is_kind

Public Member of: Event
Return Class: Boolean
Arguments:
                  Event_Type
Concurrency: Sequential

Operation Name:
  Trials

Public Member of: Event
Return Class: Trial_List
Concurrency: Sequential

Operation Name:
  set_trials

Public Member of: Event
Return Class: void
Arguments:
          Trial_List   trials
Concurrency: Sequential

Class Name: **Event_Type**

Documentation:
   Definition: A generalized contest on a particular type of
                  equipment or requiring a standard set of skills,
                  such as the balance beam or vault.

Export Control: Public
Cardinality: n
Hierarchy:
   Superclasses: none
Public Interface:
   Has-A Relationships:
         Text   description

   Operations:
         is_qualified
         description
         add_judge
         remove_judge
         qualified_judges

Private Interface:
   Has-A Relationships:
         String   name

State Machine: No
Concurrency: Sequential
Persistence: Transient

Operation Name:
  is_qualified

Public Member of: Event_Type
Arguments:
         Judge   judge
Concurrency: Sequential

Operation Name:
  description

Public Member of: Event_Type
Return Class: Text
Concurrency: Sequential

Operation Name:
  add_judge

Public Member of: Event_Type
Return Class: void
Arguments:
          Judge   judge
Concurrency: Sequential

Operation Name:
  remove_judge

Public Member of: Event_Type
Return Class: void
Arguments:
          Judge   judge
Concurrency: Sequential

Operation Name:
  qualified_judges

Public Member of: Event_Type
Return Class: Judge_List
Concurrency: Sequential

Class Name: **Gender**

Documentation:
  Definition: Represents the gender of a gymnast

Export Control: Public
Cardinality: n
Hierarchy:
  Superclasses: none
Private Interface:
  Has-A Relationships:
            Boolean   female

State Machine: No
Concurrency: Sequential
Persistence: Transient

Class Name: **Gymnast**

Documentation:
   Definition: A gymnast is an athlete that competes in a
                 league for his or her types of events. A gymnast
                 belongs to a club and competes as a club mem
                 ber. Gymnasts do not have to be in active
                 competition.

Export Control: Public
Cardinality: n
Hierarchy:
   Superclasses: Attendee
Public Interface:
   Operations:
                set_membership
                end_membership
                set_birthdate
                set_gender
                is_member
                club
                add_performance
                remove_performance
                birthdate
                gender

Private Interface:
   Has-A Relationships:
                String   name
                Gender   gender
                Address   address
                Date   birth_date

State Machine: No
Concurrency: Sequential
Persistence: Transient

Operation Name:
   set_membership

Public Member of: Gymnast
Return Class: void

Arguments:

	Team	team
	Date	start
Concurrency:		Sequential

Operation Name:
  end_membership

Public Member of:	Gymnast

Arguments:

	Team	team
	Date	end
Concurrency:		Sequential

Operation Name:
  set_birthdate

Public Member of:	Gymnast
Return Class:	void

Arguments:

	Date	birthdate
Concurrency:		Sequential

Operation Name:
  set_gender

Public Member of:	Gymnast
Return Class:	void

Arguments:

	Gender	gender
Concurrency:		Sequential

Operation Name:
  is_member

Public Member of:	Gymnast
Return Class:	Boolean

Arguments:

	Club	club
Concurrency:		Sequential

Operation Name:
  club

Public Member of:	Gymnast

Return Class: Club
Concurrency: Sequential

Operation Name:
  add_performance

Public Member of: Gymnast
Arguments:
          Trial   performance
Concurrency: Sequential

Operation Name:
  remove_performance

Public Member of: Gymnast
Arguments:
          Trial   performance
Concurrency: Sequential

Operation Name:
  birthdate

Public Member of: Gymnast
Return Class: Date
Concurrency: Sequential

Operation Name:
  gender

Public Member of: Gymnast
Return Class: Gender
Concurrency: Sequential

Class Name: **Judge**

Documentation:
  Definition: A judge is a person who rates the gymnasts
                 performances in a meet.

Export Control: Public
Cardinality: n
Hierarchy:
  Superclasses: Attendee
Public Interface:
  Has-A Relationships:
                 String   name
                 Address   address

  Operations:
                 add_qualification
                 add_assignment
                 is_assigned
                 is_qualified
                 qualifications

State Machine: No
Concurrency: Sequential
Persistence: Transient

Operation Name:
  add_qualification

Public Member of: Judge
Arguments:
        Event Type   kind
Concurrency: Sequential

Operation Name:
  add_assignment

Public Member of: Judge
Arguments:
        Event   event
Concurrency: Sequential

Operation Name:
  is_assigned

Public Member of: Judge
Arguments:
        Time_of_Day   time
Concurrency: Sequential

Operation Name:
  is_qualified

Public Member of: Judge
Arguments:
        Event Type   kind
Concurrency: Sequential

Operation Name:
  qualifications

Public Member of: Judge
Return Class: Event_Type_List
Concurrency: Sequential

Class Name: **League**

Documentation:
  Definition: A league is a collection of clubs and judges who
                participate in gymnastics meets.

Export Control: Public
Cardinality: n
Hierarchy:
  Superclasses: none
Public Interface:
  Operations:
          clubs
          judges
          gymnasts
          add_judge
          add_club
          add_gymnast

Private Interface:
  Has-A Relationships:
          Club   participants
          Judge   judges
          String   name

State Machine: No
Concurrency: Sequential
Persistence: Transient

Operation Name:
  clubs

Public Member of: League
Return Class: Club_List
Concurrency: Sequential

Operation Name:
  judges

Public Member of: League
Return Class: Judge_List
Concurrency: Sequential

Operation Name:
  gymnasts

Public Member of: League
Return Class: Gymnast_List

Concurrency: Sequential

Operation Name:
  add_judge

Public Member of: League
Arguments:
              Judge   judge
Concurrency: Sequential

Operation Name:
  add_club

Public Member of: League
Arguments:
              Club   club
Concurrency: Sequential

Operation Name:
  add_gymnast

Public Member of: League
Arguments:
              Gymnast   gymnast
Concurrency: Sequential

Class Name: **Location**

Documentation:
   Definition: Represents a location where a gymnastics meet
                  can be held.

Export Control: Public
Cardinality: n
Hierarchy:
   Superclasses: none
State Machine: No
Concurrency: Sequential
Persistence: Transient

Class Name: **Meet**

Documentation:
   Definition: A meet is a day's worth of competitions between
                teams at a given site.

Export Control: Public
Cardinality: n
Hierarchy:
   Superclasses: none
Public Interface:
   Operations:
                register_club
                date
                set_date
                set_title
                title
                set_location
                location
                get_competitions

Private Interface:
   Has-A Relationships:
                      Competition   contests
            Definition: A competition that will be run at this meet.

                  Date   date
                  String   title
                  Location   site

State Machine: No
Concurrency: Sequential
Persistence: Transient

Operation Name:
   register_club

Public Member of: Meet
Arguments:
                Club   club
Concurrency: Sequential

Operation Name:
   date

Public Member of: Meet
Return Class: Date
Concurrency: Sequential

Operation Name:
  set_date

Public Member of: Meet
Arguments:
            Date   date
Concurrency: Sequential

Operation Name:
  set_title

Public Member of: Meet
Arguments:
            String   title
Concurrency: Sequential

Operation Name:
  title

Public Member of: Meet
Return Class: String
Concurrency: Sequential

Operation Name:
  set_location

Public Member of: Meet
Arguments:
          Location   site
Concurrency: Sequential

Operation Name:
  location

Public Member of: Meet
Return Class: Location
Concurrency: Sequential

Operation Name:
  get_competitions

Public Member of: Meet
Return Class: Competition > List
Concurrency: Sequential

Class Name: **Membership**

Documentation:
Definition: Represents one gymnast's affiliation to a club.

Export Control: Public
Cardinality: n
Hierarchy:
    Superclasses: none
Public Interface:
    Operations:
            set_start
            start
            set_end
            end
            affiliation
            member

Private Interface:
    Has-A Relationships:
            Date   from
            Date   to

State Machine: No
Concurrency: Sequential
Persistence: Transient

Operation Name:
    set_start

Public Member of: Membership
Arguments:
            Date   start_date
Concurrency: Sequential

Operation Name:
    start

Public Member of: Membership
Return Class: Date
Concurrency: Sequential

Operation Name:
    set_end

Public Member of: Membership
Arguments:
            Date   end_date
Concurrency: Sequential

Operation Name:
  end

Public Member of: Membership
Return Class: Date
Concurrency: Sequential

Operation Name:
  affiliation

Public Member of: Membership
Return Class: Club
Concurrency: Sequential

Operation Name:
  member

Public Member of: Membership
Return Class: Gymnast
Concurrency: Sequential

Class Name: **Minute**

Documentation:
   Definition: Unit of time used to represent the duration of
                  events, trials, and competitions.

Export Control: Public
Cardinality: n
Hierarchy:
   Superclasses: none
State Machine: No
Concurrency: Sequential
Persistence: Transient

Class Name: **Phone_No**

Documentation:
  Definition: Represents a phone number.

Export Control: Public
Cardinality: n
Hierarchy:
  Superclasses: none
Private Interface:
  Has-A Relationships:
          String   area_code
          String   number

State Machine: No
Concurrency: Sequential
Persistence: Transient

Class Name: **Raw Score**

Documentation:
  Definition: The rating a judge gives a competitor for his or
        her trial.

        On creation, the raw_score object should be given
        the score and judge. Once a raw_score is created,
        this information cannot be changed.

Export Control: Public
Cardinality: n
Hierarchy:
  Superclasses: none
Public Interface:
  Operations:
        judge
        score

Private Interface:
  Has-A Relationships:
        Score   score
          Definition: The actual value of the score that the
                judge gave this trial

State Machine: No
Concurrency: Sequential
Persistence: Transient

Operation Name:
  judge

Public Member of: Raw Score
Return Class: Judge
Concurrency: Sequential

Operation Name:
  score

Public Member of: Raw Score
Return Class: Score
Concurrency: Sequential

Class Name: **Results_Generator**

Documentation:
   Definition: Results_Generator iterates over competition to
              get the score information to build a results
              report for a competition.

Export Control: Public
Cardinality: n
Hierarchy:
   Superclasses: none
Public Uses:

          Club
          Team
          Competition
          Event
          Meet

Public Interface:
   Operations:
        generate_report()

State Machine: No
Concurrency: Sequential
Persistence: Transient

Operation Name:
   generate_report()

Public Member of: Results_Generator
Preconditions:
   Object diagram: Scoring Report Generation

Concurrency: Sequential

Class Name: **Score**

Documentation:
  Definition: A rating given for a gymnastics trial, event,
                 competition, or meet.

Export Control: Public
Cardinality: n
Hierarchy:
  Superclasses: none
Private Interface:
  Has-A Relationships:
              Real   score

State Machine: No
Concurrency: Sequential
Persistence: Transient

Class Name: **Season**

Documentation:
  Definition: A season is a time span in which teams of the
                 league compete with each other.

Export Control: Public
Cardinality: n
Hierarchy:
  Superclasses: none
Public Interface:
  Operations:
            set_start
            start
            set_end
            end
            is_in_season
            this_days_meets

Private Interface:
  Has-A Relationships:
            Meet   meets
          Definition: A meet is a series of competitions
                        held on one day during a season.

            Date   start
            Date   end

State Machine: No
Concurrency: Sequential
Persistence: Transient

Operation Name:
  set_start

Public Member of: Season
Arguments:
            Date   start_date
Concurrency: Sequential

Operation Name:
  start

Public Member of: Season
Return Class: Date

Concurrency: Sequential

Operation Name:
  set_end

Public Member of: Season
Arguments:
         Date   end_date
Concurrency: Sequential

Operation Name:
  end

Public Member of: Season
Return Class: Date
Concurrency: Sequential

Operation Name:
  is_in_season

Public Member of: Season
Return Class: Boolean
Arguments:
         Date   date
Concurrency: Sequential

Operation Name:
  this_days_meets

Public Member of: Season
Return Class: Meet_List
Arguments:
         Date   date
Concurrency: Sequential

Class Name: **Team**

Documentation:
   Definition: A team that has registered for a particular
              competition.

Export Control: Public
Cardinality: n
Hierarchy:
   Superclasses: none
Public Interface:
   Operations:
        add_gymnast
        remove_gymnast
        members
        remove_gymnast
        set_members

State Machine: No
Concurrency: Sequential
Persistence: Transient

Operation Name:
  add_gymnast

Public Member of: Team
Arguments:
        Gymnast   member
Concurrency: Sequential

Operation Name:
  remove_gymnast

Public Member of: Team
Return Class: gymnast
Concurrency: Sequential

Operation Name:
  members

Public Member of: Team
Return Class: Gymnast_List
Concurrency: Sequential

Operation Name:
  remove_gymnast

Public Member of: Team
Return Class: void
Arguments:
          Gymnast   gymnast
Concurrency: Sequential

Operation Name:
  set_members

Public Member of: Team
Arguments:
          Team_List members
Concurrency: Sequential

Class Name: **Team_List**

Documentation:
   Definition: A list of teams instantiated from the List class
            defined in the Data_Structures category.

Export Control: Public
Cardinality: n
Hierarchy:
   Superclasses: none
   Instantiates Class: List
Private Interface:
   Has-A Relationships:
              Team

State Machine: No
Concurrency: Sequential
Persistence: Transient

Class Name: **Time_Of_Day**

Documentation:
  Definition: Represents an instant in time.

Export Control: Public
Cardinality: n
Hierarchy:
  Superclasses: none
Private Interface:
  Has-A Relationships:
                Int   hour
      Definition: An integer between 0 and 23.

                Int   minute
      Definition: An integer between 0 and 59.

State Machine: No
Concurrency: Sequential
Persistence: Transient

Class Name: **Trial**

Documentation:
   Definition: A trial is the performance of a competing
                  gymnast at a given event.

Export Control: Public
Cardinality: n
Hierarchy:
   Superclasses: none
Public Interface:
   Operations:
               add_score
               score
               judges_score
               gymnast

Private Interface:
   Has-A Relationships:
               Raw_Score scores
                  Definition:The scores the gymnast received for
                             this trial from each judge who scored
                             the trial.

State Machine: No
Concurrency: Sequential
Persistence: Transient

Operation Name:
   add_score

Public Member of: Trial
Arguments:
               Score   score
               Judge   judge
Documentation:
   Adds a score-and-judge pair to the trial's set of scores

Concurrency: Sequential

Operation Name:
   score

Public Member of: Trial
Return Class: Score

Documentation:
Computes a trial's overall score based on dropping the
highest and lowest scores and averaging the rest.

```
{
  Score net_score = scores.first();
  // Iterate over the scores and sum
  while !(scores.done())
  {
    net_score = net_score + scores.next();
  }
  // Throw out the low and high score
  net_score = net_score - (scores.min() +
scores.max() );
  // Average by scores used
  net_score = net_score /(scores.length -s 2 );
  return net_score;
};
```

Concurrency: Sequential

Operation Name:
  judges_score

Public Member of: Trial
Return Class: Score
Arguments:
              Judge   judge
Concurrency: Sequential

Operation Name:
  gymnast

Public Member of: Trial
Return Class: Gymnast
Concurrency: Sequential

Appendix B

■

Class Diagrams

■

Object Diagrams

■

Interaction Diagrams

■

Module Diagrams

■

Process Diagrams

■

State Diagrams

THE BOOCH NOTATION is a standard notation for object-oriented analysis and design. The Booch notation answers the following questions during analysis and design:

- What classes exist and how are those classes related?

- How are individual objects structured, and what mechanisms are used to specify how societies of objects collaborate?

- Where should each class and object be defined?

- To what processor should a process be allocated and, for a given processor, how should its multiple processes be scheduled?

- What are the valid states of a class or system?

These six diagrams form the notation of the Booch method:

- Class diagrams

- Object diagrams

- Interaction diagrams

- Module diagrams

- Process diagrams

- State transition diagrams

CLASS DIAGRAMS

A CLASS DIAGRAM shows the existence of classes and class categories,and their relationships in the logical view of a system.A single class diagram represents one view into the class structure of a system.

Class diagrams can contain classes, class categories, or a mixture of the two. You can create one or more class diagrams to depict the categories and classes at the top level of your design or to depict a portion of the system's class structure.

You can use class diagrams to

- Show common roles and responsibilities of the entities that provide the system's behavior during analysis

- Capture the structure of the classes that form the system's architecture during design

Classes rarely stand alone but instead collaborate with other classes in a variety of ways. The essential connections among classes include association, inherits, has, and uses relationships.

Class Category

Class categories serve to partition the logical model of a system. They are clusters of highly related classes that are themselves cohesive but loosely coupled relative to other such clusters. You can use class categories to group classes and other class categories.

While most object-oriented programming languages do not provide support for this concept, using class categories in a class diagram allows you to express and preserve important architectural elements of the system design. You can capture a high-level design of the system by creating a class diagram that consists only of class categories.

You can draw class categories only in class diagrams.

Class

A class captures the common structure and common behavior of a set of objects. A class is an abstraction of real-world items. When these items exist in the real world, they are instances of the class, known as objects.

For each class that has significant event-ordered behavior, you can create a state diagram associated with it.

The key attributes, operations, and constraints of a class can be listed inside the class icon.

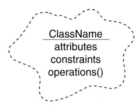

Parameterized Class

A parameterized class is a template for creating any number of instantiated classes that follow its format. A parameterized class declares formal parameters. You can use other classes, objects, operations, or a combination of these items as parameters. You cannot use the parameterized class itself as a parameter. You must instantiate a parameterized class before you can create its objects.

In its simplest form, you use parameterized classes to build container classes.

The C++, Eiffel, and Ada languages support parameterized classes.

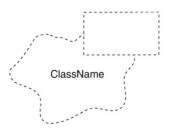

Instantiated Class

You create an instantiated class by supplying actual values for the formal parameters of the parameterized class. This instantiation process forms a concrete class in the family of the parameterized class. You must place the instantiated class at the source end of an instantiates relationship that points to the corresponding parameterized class.

An instantiated class whose actual parameters differ from other concrete classes in the family of the parameterized class forms a new class in the family.

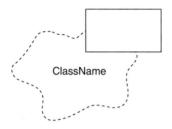

ClassName

Metaclass

A metaclass is a class whose instances are classes rather than objects. Metaclasses provide operations for initializing class variables and serve as repositories to hold class variables where a single value will be required by all objects of a class.

Smalltalk and CLOS support the use of metaclasses. C++ does not directly support metaclasses.

ClassName

Class Utility

A class utility is a set of operations that provide additional functions for classes. You can use class utilities to

- Denote one or more free subprograms

- Name a class that only has class instance variables

Parameterized Class Utility

A parameterized class utility is a set of operations or functions that are not associated with a higher-level class (free subprograms) and are defined in terms of formal parameters. You can use a parameterized class utility as a template for creating instantiated class utilities.

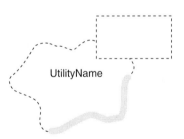

Instantiated Class Utility

An instantiated class utility is created by substituting actual values
for the formal parameters of a parameterized class utility.

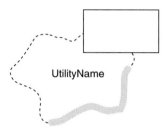

UtilityName

Association Relationship

An association represents a semantic connection between two classes. Associations are bidirectional; they are the most general of all relationships and the most semantically weak.

During analysis, you will initially identify general dependencies
between classes. As your model evolves, you may change your initial associations to more semantically precise relationships, such as
aggregation relationships.

ClassA   ClassB

Attributed Association

An attributed relationship models properties associated with an association. To indicate the attributes of an association, you can use a dashed line to link the association to it's properties. The properties must be represented by a class.

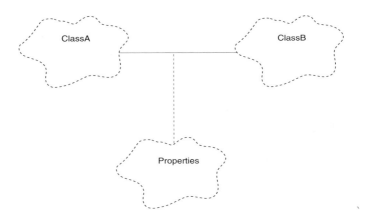

Has Relationship

Use the has relationship to show a whole-and-part relationship between two classes. This relationship is also known as an aggregation relationship.

The class at the source end of the has relationship is sometimes called the aggregate class. An instance of the aggregate class is an aggregate object. The class at the target end of the has relationship is the part whose instances are contained or owned by the aggregate object.

You can use the has relationship to show that the aggregate object is physically constructed from other objects or that it logically contains another object. The aggregate object has ownership of its parts.

The circle end designates the source end, and the other end is the target class.

Uses Relationship

You can draw a uses relationship between two classes to show that the source class depends on the target class to provide certain services, such as

- The source class accesses a value (constant or variable) defined in the target class

- Operations of the source class invoke operations of the target class

- Operations of the source class have signatures whose return class or arguments are instances of the target class

The circle end designates the source class, and the other end is the target class.

Inherits Relationship

An inherits relationship between classes shows that the subclass shares the structure or behavior defined in one or more superclasses. You can use an inherits relationship to show an is-a relationship between classes.

The arrowhead points toward the base class.

Instantiates Relationship

An instantiates relationship represents the act of substituting actual values for the parameters of a parameterized class or parameterized class utility to create a specialized version of the more general item. In most cases, you will also draw a uses relationship between the instantiated class and another concrete class used as an actual parameter.

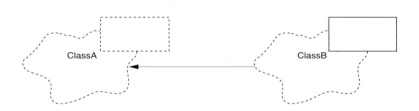

The arrowhead points toward the parameterized class or parameterized class utility.

Meta Relationship

You can use the meta relationship to show the connection between a class and its metaclass.

Abstract Adornment

The abstract adornment identifies a class that serves as a base class, defining operations and state that will be inherited by subclasses. An abstract class has no instances.

You must designate a class as abstract if it has one or more abstract operations.

The abstract adornment is the letter "A" inside a triangle.

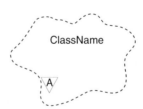

Static Adornment

You can use the static adornment on a has relationship to specify that the source class, not the source's instances, owns the target class. In C++, the static adornment represents a static data member, and in Smalltalk it represents a class variable.

The static adornment is the letter "S" inside a triangle.

Friend Adornment

You can use the friend adornment to designate that the target class has granted rights to a source class to access its nonpublic parts. The friend adornment may be applied to the target end of uses and inherits relationships.

The friend adornment is the letter "F" inside a triangle.

Virtual Adornment

You can use the virtual adornment to designate a shared base class in a multiple inheritance situation. Applying the virtual adornment to the inherits relationship for a subclass ensures that only one copy of the base class will be inherited by descendants of the subclass. The virtual adornment may be applied only to the inherits relationship.

The virtual adornment is the letter "V" inside a triangle.

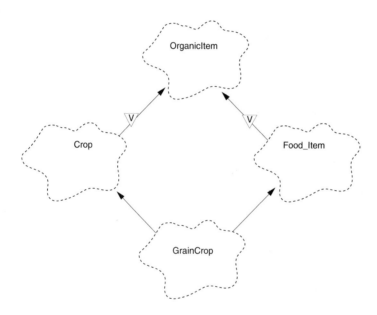

Cardinality Adornment

You can indicate cardinality for classes and relationships.

- When you apply a cardinality adornment to a class, you are indicating the number of instances allowed for that class.

- When you apply a cardinality adornment to a relationship, you are indicating the number of links between the instances of the source class and the instances of the target class.

Valid Values You can use the following cardinality values for either class or relationship cardinalilty.

Value	Description
1	One instance
n	Unlimited number
0..n	Zero or more
1..n	One or more
0..1	Zero or one
< literal >	Exact number
< literal >..n	Exact number or more
< literal >..< literal >	Specified range

Class Cardinality You can specify cardinality for a class or parameterized class. The default cardinality is n.

Relationship Cardinality You can specify cardinality for association, has, and uses relationships. The default cardinality is unspecified.

Cardinality values for a relationship are shown at the applicable end(s) of the relationship.

Roles, Keys, and Constraints

The role of an abstraction denotes the purpose or capacity wherein one class associates with another. The role of a class is placed as a textual adornment on any association, placed adjacent to the class identified by the role.

A key is a value that uniquely identifies a single target object. Keys are surrounded by square brackets.

A constraint is an expression of some semantic condition that must be preserved. Expressions are surrounded by braces.

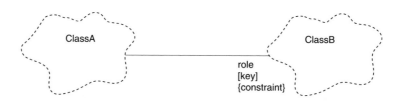

By-Value Adornment

Apply the by-value adornment to a has relationship between two classes to show that an instance of one class physically contains an instance of another class. The by-value adornment specifices that the lifetime of an instance of the target end of the relationship is dependent on the lifetime of the source end of the relationship.

The by-value adornment is a black square at the target end of a has relationship.

By-Reference Adornment

Apply the by-reference adornment to a has relationship between two classes to show that each instance of one class has a pointer or reference within it to an instance of another class.

Classes in a has by-reference relationship represent data that can be manipulated by more than one class. Because storage for the target class is not maintained by the source class, the instance of the target class can be altered or deleted while the reference to it still exists. Therefore, its lifetime is not dependent on the lifetime of the source class.

The by-reference adornment is an open square at the target end of a has relationship.

Access Adornments

You can use access adornments to specify the type of access allowed between classes: public, private, protected, or implementation.

You can apply the access adornments to has, uses, or inherits relationships. You cannot apply any of the access adornments to instantiates or meta relationships.

Access adornments are cross bars placed at the source end of relationships:

- Public (default)

- Protected

- Private

- Implementation

Public Public access means that the members of a class are accessible to all other classes. This is the default access.

Protected Protected access means that the members of a class are accessible only to subclasses, friends, or to the class itself.

    The protected access adornment is one cross bar at the source end of the relationship. The following figure shows a protected inheritance relationship.

    You can apply the protected access adornment with has, uses, and inherits relationships.

Private Private access means that the members of a class are accessible only to the class itself or to its friends.

    The private access adornment is two crossbars at the source end of the relationship. The following figure shows a private inheritance relationship.

Implementation Implementation access means that the class is accessible only by the implementation of the class containing the class. It might be declared as a local variable in one of the source classes operations.

The implementation access adornment is three crossbars at the source end of the relationship. The following figure shows a uses for implementation relationship.

OBJECT DIAGRAMS

Use object diagrams to show the existence of objects and their links in a logical model of a system. An object diagram is one view into the system's object structure. You can use the diagram to show a portion of the system's object structure or to show the entire structure. Object diagrams highlight the important mechanisms that manipulate the key abstractions illustrated in the model's class diagrams.

Object diagrams contain objects and their links. Object diagrams can also contain simple class instances, class utility instances, and metaclass instances. These class instances are object-like things that operate upon other objects and may, in turn, be operated upon.

You can use object diagrams to

- Indicate the semantics of scenarios during analysis

- Show the semantics of mechanisms in the logical design of the system

- Validate the model during analysis and design

Use object diagrams as the primary vehicle to describe scenarios that express your decisions about the behavior of the system.

Object

An object has state, behavior, and identity. The structure and behavior of similar objects are defined in their common class. Each object in a diagram indicates some instance of a class.

The object icon is similar to a class icon except that it has a solid line as a boundary.

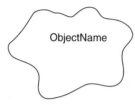

If you have multiple objects that are instances of the same class, you can use the multiple objects icon.

Link

Objects interact through their links to other objects. A link is an instance of an association, or of a has relationship, analogous to an object being an instance of a class.

A link may exist between two objects, including class utilities and metaclasses, only if there is a relationship between their corresponding classes. The existence of a relationship between two classes symbolizes a path of communication between instances of the classes: one object may send messages to another. All classes implicitly have an association to themselves; therefore, an object may be linked to itself.

The link is a straight line between objects or objects and class instances in an object diagram.

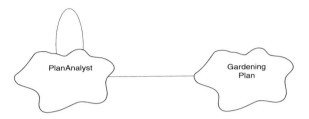

Message

Objects can send various types of messages to one another. Messages can include system signals, IPC messages, messages to and from external objects, and, most commonly, calls to the receiving objects. Message-passing between two objects is generally in one direction; it can also be bi-directional. Data can flow in both directions.

Each of the following message types has its own synchronization adornment:

- Simple

- Synchronous

- Balking

- Timeout

- Asynchronous

The default synchronization for a message is simple.

Visibility Adornments

Object visibility is the ability of one object to see another object. If visibility is an important detail in your software model, you can use visibility adornments to show these details in an object diagram.

You can specify object visibility as shared or unshared. Shared visibility indicates structural sharing of an object; the shared object's state can be altered via more than one path. Unshared visibility represents unique access given to the source object.

An object visibility adornment is a letter inside a box placed at the target end of the link. Each letter identifies the type of visibility used. The adornment box is either open or filled:

- For shared visibility, the adornment is an open square.

- For unshared visibility, the adornment is a filled square.

The visibility adornments are described below.

Field Visibility You can use the field visibility adornment to indicate that the source object operates on one of its own data members; that is, the target is visible because it is a field of the source. The class of the source object has a data member with the type of the target object, and one of the operations of the class acts upon this field.

Parameter Visibility You can use the parameter visibility adornment to indicate that the target object is visible to the source object because it is a parameter for one of the source's operations.

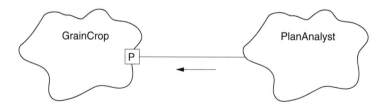

Local Visibility You can use the local visibility adornment to indicate that the target object is local to an operation of the source object.

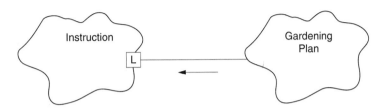

Global Visibility You can use the global visibility adornment to indicate that the target is global to the source object.

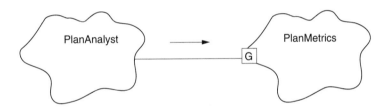

Synchronization Adornments
Each synchronization adornment represents one or more messages passed between two objects. These adornments indicate the direction of message passing and point toward the target object.

You can label synchronization adornments to identify the operations being invoked. The adornment labels can contain identifiers or valid operators for a programming language.

The synchronization adornments are described in the following sections.

Simple For messages with a single thread of control, one object sends a message to a passive object.

The simple synchronization adornment is a small, straight arrow.

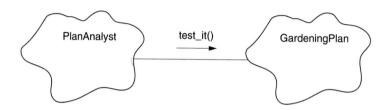

Synchronous In synchronous messages, the operation proceeds only when the source sends a message to the target and the target accepts the message. The source runs until it sends the message; it then waits for the target to accept it. The source continues to wait until the message is accepted.

The synchronous adornment is a small straight arrow with an "X" behind the arrowhead.

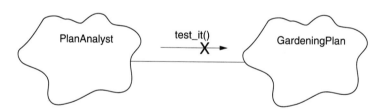

Balking In balking synchronization, the source can pass a message only if the target is immediately ready to accept the message. The source abandons the message if the target is not ready.

The balking synchronization adornment is an arrow that loops back to point toward the source object.

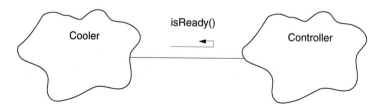

Timeout In timeout synchronization, the source abandons a message if the target cannot handle the message within a specified amount of time.

The timeout synchronization adornment is an arrow with a clock icon behind the arrowhead.

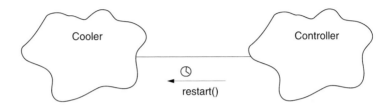

Asynchronous Asynchronous communication occurs when the source sends a message to the target for processing and continues to execute its code without waiting for or relying on the target's receipt of the message.

The asynchronous adornment is an arrow with a modified arrowhead.

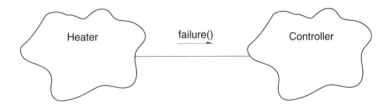

Roles, Keys, and Constraints

The section on class diagrams mentioned that associations may be adorned with roles, keys, and constraints. These adornments can be restated on the corresponding link between two objects.

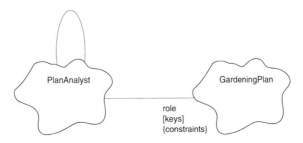

INTERACTION DIAGRAMS

An interaction diagram, like an object diagram, is used to trace the execution of a scenario. An interaction diagram is another way of representing the information on an object diagram. It is easier to read the relative order of messages on an interaction diagram. Unlike object diagrams, an interaction diagram does not show links, attribute values, or visibility.

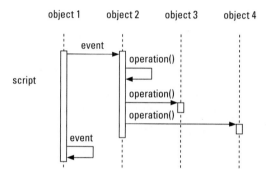

MODULE DIAGRAMS

A module diagram shows the allocation of classes and objects to modules in the physical model of the system. You can use a module diagram to show all or part of the module architecture for a system. During design, use module diagrams to show dependencies between modules.

Module diagrams contain the following elements:

- Subsystems

- Package Specification

- Package Body

- Main Program

- Dependencies

These module types are not supported by all languages. For example, Ada supports all of the module types, C + + only supports the concept of simple files, and Smalltalk does not contain the concept of a module at all.

You can create a special type of module diagram that contains only subsystems (a subsystem diagram) to show the high-level architecture of the physical model.

Module diagrams are unnecessary for languages that do not support modules, such as Smalltalk.

Subsystems

Subsystems represent clusters of logically related modules. Subsystems parallel the role played by class categories for class diagrams.

Subsystems allow you to partition the physical model of the system. Each subsystem can contain modules and other subsystems. Each module in your system must reside in a single subsystem or at the top level of your model. Subsystems frequently represent major functional components of your system.

By convention, every module contained in a subsystem is public unless you explicitly define it to be restricted to implementation access.

A subsystem can have dependencies with other subsystems and modules; a module can have a dependency with a subsystem.

The subsystem icon is a rectangle with rounded corners.

Package Specification

In C++, you can use the package specification to represent the .h file.

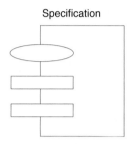

Package Body

In C++, you can use the package body to represent the .cpp file.

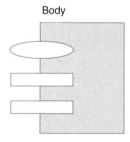

Main Program

This module represents a file that contains the root of a program. For example, in C++ this module may represent a .cpp file that contains the definition of the privileged nonmember function called main.

You will normally identify only one main program module per program.

The main program icon looks like this.

Main

Dependencies

The dependency is the only relationship that makes sense between two entities in a module diagram. Dependencies in the module diagram represent compilation dependencies. For example, in C++, compilation dependencies are indicated by #include statements; in Ada, they are indicated by with clauses.

Dependency is represented by a line with an arrowhead.

stack.h   stack.cpp

PROCESS DIAGRAMS

A process diagram shows how processes are allocated to processors in the physical model of the system. The process diagram is equal to one view into the process structure of the system. A process diagram can show all or part of the system architecture. You can have only one process diagram per model.

During design, use a process diagram to show the physical collection of processors and devices that serve as the platform for execution of your system.

A process diagram contains

- Processors

- Devices

- Connections

Processor

A processor is a piece of hardware capable of executing programs.

The icon for a processor is a shaded box.

Device

A device is a piece of hardware that has no computing power. Each device must have a name. Device names can be generic, such as modem or terminal.

The icon for a device is a box.

Connection

A connection represents some type of hardware coupling between two entities. An entity is either a processor or a device. The hardware coupling can be direct, such as an RS232 cable, or indirect, such as satellite-to-ground communication. Connections are usually bidirectional. They can be labelled with an appropriate name.

The icon for a connection is a straight line.

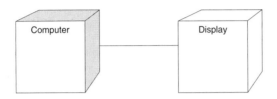

STATE DIAGRAMS

Each class can have an associated state diagram that shows the event-ordered behavior of the instances of the class. You should create a state diagram only for those classes that have significant event-ordered behavior.

You can use a state diagram to show

- State space of a given time

- Events that cause a transition from one state to another

- Actions that result from a state change

State diagrams contain:

- States

- State transitions

Each state diagram must have exactly one start state. You can also designate a stop state.

State

The state of an object represents the cumulative history of its behavior. State encompasses all of the object's static properties and the current values of each property.

All instances of the same class live in the same state space.

The state icon is a rounded rectangle with the state name.

Start State A start state is a special state that explicitly shows the beginning of the state machine. You can have exactly one start state in each state diagram.

The start state icon is a solid circle with an arrow.

Stop State A stop state represents a final or terminal state of a system. Draw a stop state when you want to explicitly show the end of the state machine. Transitions can only occur into an end state; once the state machine stops, it goes out of existence.

Normally, you can assume that the state machine associated with a class will go out of existence when its enclosing object is destroyed and, therefore, never reaches an end state. However, you can use an end state to explicitly show the end, if necessary.

The stop state is a circle enclosing a solid circle with an arrow.

State Transition

A state transition is a change of state caused by an event. Use state transitions to connect two states in a state diagram or show state transitions from a state to itself. You can show one or more state transitions from a state as long as each transition is unique.

The icon for a state transition is a line with an arrowhead pointing toward the next state.

You can label each state transition with the name of at least one event that causes the state transition.

An event label is one of the following:

- Symbolic name

- Object name

- Name of an operation

Nesting

The ability to nest states gives depth to state transition diagrams. Enclosing states are called superstates, and nested states are called substates. If the system is in a particular superstate, then it must be in exactly one of it's substates.

State transitions can take the following forms:

- From one state to a peer state

- Directly to a substate, or directly from a substate

- Directly from a supersate, which means that the state transition applies to every substate of the superstate

- Directly to a superstate with substates, which means transitioning to the superstates default state.

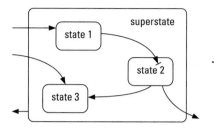

History

Often when **transitioning** directly to a state with substates, you want to return to the most recently visited state. These semantics may be indicated with the history icon, shown as the letter H inside a circle.

Index

■ (black squares), 186, 192
{} (braces), 186
| (one crossbar), 188
|| (two crossbars), 188–189
||| (three crossbars), 189
_ (line), 191
☐ (open squares), 187, 192
[] (square brackets), 186

abstract adornment ⩔ , 182
abstraction reuse, 87, 88
abstractions, 3, 9
  data dictionary, 30–31
  defined, 14
  domain analysis, 9
  identifying, 29–30
  key, 11, 33
access adornments, 187–189
access control, 119–121
addresses, 64
adornments, 182–189
aggregations, 178
  defined, 52
  defining, 44
  notation, 178, 179
algorithms, 114–115
analysis. *See* domain analysis
architectural descriptions, 12
architectural reuse, 87, 88
architecture (software)
  defined, 94
  defining, 89, 97
  determining, 12–13
  importance, 85–86
architecture (system), 12, 199–201
associations
  attributed, 179
  defined, 52
  defining, 43
  navigation paths, 116
  notation, 179, 185
asynchronous adornment ——⬙ , 195
attributed association, 178
attributes, 30, 31. *See also* inheritance
  approaches to, 64–66
  assigning, 66–67
  defined, 14, 71
  defining, 63
  finding, 10
  types, 63
attribution process, 63

balking synchronization adornment
  ⬙⁻ , 194
base class, 182
bidirectionality, 43, 191
Booch method
  advantages, 4
  definition, 3–6
  iterative aspects, 78–80
  notation, 173–204
  steps, 6–13
by-reference adornment ☐ , 187
by-value adornment ■ , 186

candidate classes, 29
cardinality
  defined, 52
  defining, 48–51
cardinality adornment, 184–185
class cardinality, 185
class categories, 86
  defined, 94
  defining, 98–104
  notation, 174
class-category diagrams, 12, 93
class diagrams
  attributes, 63
  cardinality, 49, 50
  defined, 14
  domain analysis, 10
  notation, 173–189
  system design, 12, 93–94
  types and, 64
class icon, 175
class specifications
  adding operations, 55, 57
  complete, 94
  defined, 14
  domain analysis, 10
  system design, 12
class structure, 43
class utility, 177
class variables, 176
classes
  access to, 119–121
  attributes, 66–67
  candidate, 29
  characteristics, 31–32
  defined, 14
  defining, 10, 29–32
  filtering, 30
  general. *See* superclasses
  key, 10, 29
  logical, 29, 32

naming, 31–32
notation, 174–175
operations for, 55–59
properties. *See* attributes
relationships, 43
specialized. *See* subclasses
as types, 64
cloud compartment, 63
cohesion, 31, 103
connections (hardware), 201
constraints, 180, 189
container classes, 118, 175
containment, 116–117
  adornments, 186–187
  defined, 121
control classes
  adding, 110, 111–112
  defined, 121
cost-effectiveness, 85
coupling, 31, 103, 104
customers' roles
  domain analysis, 11
  requirements analysis, 7, 19
  system design, 13

data dictionary
  building, 30–31
  defined, 14
  domain analysis, 10
  types in, 64
data types. *See* types
database managers, 97
date ranges, 64
dates, 64
default access, 188
default synchronization, 181
definitions. *See* semantic definitions
dependencies module, 197, 199
dependency. *See* coupling
design. *See* system design
development schedule, 87
device interfaces, 97
devices, 200
dictionary. *See* data dictionary
difficulty factors, 69
documentation. *See also* class specifications; relationship
  specifications
  in system design, 87
domain analysis
  attributes, 63–66
  classes, 29–32
  during system design, 86
  inheritance, 67
  iterating, 77–80
  operations, 55–60
  overview, 6, 9–11
  relationships, 43–52
  reuse in, 88
  validating, 75–77

domain experts, 21

encapsulation, 119
end users. *See* customers' roles
event labels, 203
executable releases, 4
  building, 21
  defined, 14
  defining, 13, 85
  descriptions, 12
  developing, 13, 92, 109–121
  planning, 13, 87, 89–91
  system design, 109–111
  testing, 13, 92
  validating, 109
exported classes, 102
  defined, 105
expressions, 186

field visibility adornment Ⓕ, 192
formulas, 114
friend adornment ▽, 183
friend classes, 119
functions
  general, 33
  key, 6

generalized classes. *See* supertypes
gestalt design, 79–80
global class categories, 102
global visibility adornment Ⓖ, 193
GUIs (graphical user interfaces), 32, 86, 98
gymnastics system
  abstractions, 33–37
  attributes, 65, 66
  cardinality diagram, 50
  charter statement, 24
  class categories, 99–101
  class diagram, 38–39, 76
  class specifications, 38–39
  data dictionary, 40
  executable release, 93
  listing operations, 59
  object-scenario diagrams, 75, 76
  problem statement, 22–23
  relationships, 43, 44, 45, 47–48
  reports generation, 112–113
  score computations, 114–115
  superclasses and subclasses, 68–70
  system charter, 24
  system function statement, 24–25
  visibility in, 102–103

has relationships. *See* aggregations
history, 204

implementation, 86, 88, 112–115
implementation access adornment
‖‖, 189

imported classes, 102
defined, 105
information hiding, 119
information sources, 19–21
inheritance, 10
defined, 14, 71
defining, 67–68
inherits relationship, 181, 183
input switches, 55
instantiated class utility, 177–178
instantiated classes, 118, 176
defined, 122
instantiates relationship, 181
interaction diagrams, 196
interfaces
device, 97
user, 90
is-a relationship, 181
iterative approaches, 5–6
domain analysis, 10, 11, 77–80
system design, 13, 86–87

key (adj.), defined, 33
keys, 186, 195

labeling messages, 57
links, 190–191
lists, linked, 32
local classes, 102
local visibility adornment ⊡ , 193
logical structure, 6, 86

main program module, 198–199
maintenance, 86
mandatory relationships, 49, 50
mechanism reuse, 88
mechanisms, key, 11
messages, 191
meta relationship, 182
metaclass, 176
models, 4
defined, 15
producing, 4, 9
validating, 75–77
module diagrams, 196–199
multiple objects icon, 190
multiprocessor interfaces, 97

naming
classes, 31
events, 203
operations, 55
relationships, 44
natural language, 30
navigation paths, 43
adding, 111, 116
nesting, 203
nouns, 29–30

object diagrams, 56–57, 189–195

defined, 15
domain analysis, 10
system design, 12, 94
object icon, 190
object-oriented design methods, 4, 86–87
objects, 3, 30, 174
identifying, 9
operating system, 97
operations, 9, 10
assigning, 55–60
defined, 15
implementing, 112–115
optional relationships, 49
output samples, 23
overloaded terms, 30, 35

package body module, 198
package specification module, 198
parameter visibility adornment ⓟ , 192
parameterized class utility, 177
parameterized classes, 118
defined, 122
notation, 175
parsing, 29–30
participants
domain analysis, 11
requirements analysis, 9
system design, 13
partitions. *See* class categories
physical structure, 6, 86
porting systems, 85, 101
private access, 119
defined, 122
private access adornment ‖ , 188–189
problem domain, 9
identifying abstractions in, 29–30
learning, 19–21
process diagrams, 199–200
processors, 200
properties. *See* attributes
protected access, 119
defined, 122
protected access adornment | , 188
public access, 119, 188
defined, 122

quantity. *See* cardinality

Rational Rose definitions
access control, 120
attributes, 67
cardinality, 51
class categories, 101
class specifications, 38–39
containment, 117
inheritance, 70
key classes, 38
object-scenario diagrams, 57
operations, 56, 115
relationship specifications, 46

relationships, 46
  visibility, 104
relationship specifications, 46, 51
  access control, 120
relationships, 30. *See* also aggregations;
associations
  cardinality, 48–51, 185
  classes, 43–44
  defined, 15
  defining, 10, 47–48
  implementing, 116–117
  mandatory, 49, 50
  naming, 44
  optional, 49
releases. <u>See</u> executable releases
requirements analysis
  information sources, 19–21
  overview, 6–9
  role of, 19
reuse, 87–88, 118
rigidity, 104
risk areas, 90
roles, 186, 195
round-trip gestalt design, 79–80

scripts, 56
semantic definitions, 9, 11, 31–32
  sequence numbers, 56
service software, 97–98
simple synchronization adornment
      ⟶ , 194
software engineers' roles
  domain analysis, 11
  system analysis, 13
software-development methods, 3, 78–79
source classes, 45, 48, 116–117, 180
specialized classes. *See* subclasses
specifications. *See also* class specifications;
    relationship specifications
  in system design, 12
start state, 202
state diagrams, 201–204
state transitions, 203
static adornment ⟨S⟩ , 183
stop state, 202
strings, 64
subclasses
  defined, 71
  identifying, 69
  inheritance and, 68, 181
subsets. *See* executable releases
substates, 204
subsystems module, 197
subtypes, 31
superclasses
  defined, 71
  identifying, 68
  inheritance and, 68, 181
superstates, 203
supertypes, 31

synchronization, 191
synchronization adornments, 193–195
synchronous adornment —×—► , 194
synonyms, 30, 34, 36
system charter, 8, 19
  defined, 25
system design
  defining, 85
  overview, 6, 11–13
  principles, 85–88
  products, 93–94
  steps, 88–93
system domain, 9
system function statement, 8, 19
  defined, 25
  purpose, 24
system integration, 87

target classes, 45, 48, 116–117, 179–180
testing, 13, 87, 91
time ranges, 64
timeout synchronization adornment
  ◄ ⊙ , 195
types, 10, 64, 69, 90. *See also* classes

use case analysis, 7
use cases, 6–7
  defined, 15
  key, 7, 8
  modeling, 56–58
  system function statement, 24, 25
user interface, 90
uses relationship, 58, 103, 180, 185
utilities, 89, 177–178

validating, 10
  design decisions, 12
  domain analysis, 77–79
  executable releases, 109
virtual adornment ⟨V⟩ , 184
visibility
  defined, 105
  defining, 101–104
visibility adornments, 191–192

waterfall model of software
development, 6, 78